Praise for *The Essential Laws of Fearless Living*

"In *Fearless Living*, Guy Finley brilliantly describes the most import key to the breakthrough life. Let go of all the negatives, and turn over the fears to God. What happens afterward is that we are free to follow our deepest intuitions with courage. A valuable, step-by-step book."
—JAMES REDFIELD, author of *The Celestine Prophecy*

"*The Essential Laws of Fearless Living*: How could so much knowledge be packed into such a little book? For anyone looking for a rich path to a courageous life, this book is for you!"
—ANNA DARRAH, Director of Acquisitions, Spiritual Cinema Circle

"I have known and interviewed many who offer insight into human development. No one does it with the kind of grace, intelligence, and love as my friend Guy Finley. This book is his latest gift to all people seeking to overcome fear and live more fulfilling lives. Guy is an extraordinary person who reminds us just how special we are."
—JORDAN RICH, WBZ Boston

"Guy Finley's cutting edge work in *Fearless Living* takes us beyond illusion and taps into the pathway of 'Unbridled Living.' A must read for all!"
—MICHAEL DRESSER, host of the nationally syndicated *Michael Dresser Show*

"A must have book! Every page is filled with timeless wisdom presented in everyday language that shows people, step by step, how to burst through the illusion of fear and be truly free."
—LINDA MACKENZIE, C.H.T., Ph.D., founder, *HealthyLife.net*, All Positive Talk & Music Radio

"Guy Finley is a prophetic teacher whose focus is on the Light within each human being. His message is that when we direct our thoughts toward this Light we can live without fear and negativity. In this book, he provides a lesson plan for self-empowerment and transformation."
—MARY CARROLL NELSON, author of
Freedom and Joy—The Teachings of Dᴏ

"A book that encourages our self-examination of thinking, conscience, and behavior—an essential step for each of us to hear the call for our important contributions at this time in history. His questions serve as a mirror of what stands in our way. The wisdom shared reminds us of the powerful truth—'all is within.'"

> —DEBBE KENNEDY, founder, Global Dialogue Center and Leadership Solutions Companies and author of *Putting Our Differences to Work: The Fastest Way to Innovation, Leadership and High Performance*

"The gems of wisdom in *Fearless Living* liberate you to embrace and embody the Light of Your True Self and freely shine the love and peace at your core."

> —ALISSA LUKARA, author of *Riding Grace: A Triumph of the Soul* and president of *Lifechallenges.org*

"Guy Finley's visionary wisdom in *The Essential Laws of Fearless Living* speaks to the deep places within us. Read slowly. Absorb every word. This work redefines limitless living. Gems of Truth are awaiting your discovery.

> —LARRY JAMES, author of *How to Really Love the One You're With*

"In his own inimitable and inspiring way, Guy Finley reminds us of the power we possess within. Whatever you may be wrestling with in daily life, *The Essential Laws of Fearless Living* provides the wisdom to cut through to the heart of the matter. This book is the best of Guy's writings to date because it encompasses the entire pantheon of his vast resource of aphorisms and insights. Anyone on the path, or off it, must get this book and *read* it!"

> —MICHAEL TOMS, founding CEO, New Dimensions Media; author of *An Open Life: Joseph Campbell in Conversation with Michael Toms*, and coauthor of *True Work: Doing What You Love and Loving What You Do*

"Wise, insightful, full of wisdom. This book can soothe the soul and allow healing into a hurting heart. Powerful."

> —DANIEL G. AMEN, MD, *New York Times* bestselling author of *Change Your Brain, Change Your Life*

"This truly is the best of Guy Finley... beautifully designed by a modern master to bring out the best in *you!*"

— PEGGY McCOLL, *New York Times* bestselling author of *Your Destiny Switch*

"Guy Finley's *Essential Laws of Fearless Living* is a masterwork of eternal value. If you purchase only one book by Guy Finley, let this be the one... it *will* transform your life!"

— SARA ROBINSON, author of *Refuge,* founder of Conscious Creating

"In his newest book, Guy Finley continues to address the deepest matters of life... his words and profound wisdom will jolt you into that breathless and boundless present-moment experience where the 'Isness' of real life truly begins."

— CAROLYN R. CRAFT, radio host/Unity minister

"*The Essential Laws of Fearless Living* illuminates what is possible for us to become in this time of shattering changes. It is a map to what I call 'Living Successfully.' It's not surprising to me that Guy Finley was the man to pass it along to us."

— BOB KEETON, host/producer, "Living Successfully"

"The problems that most people have in life are not from 'lack of power' but from the abuse/misuse of the power that they already have. Mr. Finley shows us how to nip this in the bud, by raising our altitude to the right level. This seemingly simple act transforms our minds and outer lives."

— JOSEPH POLANSKY, *Diamond Fire* magazine

"The works of Guy Finley demonstrate a far greater purpose for you and me and the human race than simply making ourselves comfortable; they challenge, provoke, and finally compel us to get to the real Heart of the matter: A place where the True Comfort of Reality exists."

— SCOTT CLUTHE, executive producer/host, *Positively Incorrect!*

"Guy explains the difference between really living and just going through the motions, and urges us never to settle for less than the real thing. If where you are in life is not where you want to be, Guy will help you close the gap."

— DR. ARRON GROW, *Personal Best Radio*

"Guy Finley raises our thoughts to the higher octaves of harmony where we can transform our lives into clear and focused vessels of expression, creativity, and health. *The Essential Laws of Fearless Living* brings us multiple ways to awaken our potential with what we are today."
—DON CAMPBELL, author of *The Mozart Effect* and *The Harmony of Health*

"In *The Essential Laws of Fearless Living*, Guy Finley has compiled compelling, insightful messages that invite us to let go of fear and rejoin Love. Thank you for leading the way, Guy!"
—ILENE L. DILLON, M.S.W., *Full Power Living* radio host, *www.emotionalpro.com*

"If you are seeking personal or spiritual fulfillment, it doesn't get any better than Guy Finley's *Essential Laws of Fearless Living*. Read it. Internalize it. And then enjoy it. This information has given me everything I have today."
—BOB PROCTOR, author of *You Were Born Rich*, as seen in the movie *The Secret*

THE ESSENTIAL LAWS OF
FEARLESS
LIVING

THE ESSENTIAL LAWS OF
FEARLESS
LIVING

FIND THE POWER
TO NEVER FEEL
POWERLESS AGAIN

Guy Finley

Foreword by Dr. Ellen Dickstein

WEISER BOOKS
San Francisco, CA / Newburyport, MA

First published in 2008 by
Red Wheel/Weiser, LLC
With offices at:
500 Third Street, Suite 230
San Francisco, CA 94107
www.redwheelweiser.com

ISBN: 978-1-57863-427-9

LIBRARY OF CONGRESS CATALOGING-IN-PUBLICATION DATA
Finley, Guy, 1949-
  The essential laws of fearless living : find the power to never feel powerless again / Guy Finley ; foreword by Ellen Dickstein.
    p. cm.
  ISBN 978-1-57863-427-9 (alk. paper)
  1. Self-actualization (Psychology) 2. Success—Psychological aspects. I. Title.
  BF637.S4F545 2008
  158.1—dc22   2007051465

Cover and text design by Maxine Ressler
Typeset in Adobe Garamond and Baily Sans ITC
Cover photograph © AVTG/iStockphoto
Printed in the United States of America
TS
10 9 8 7 6 5 4

The paper used in this publication meets the minimum requirements of the American National Standard for Information Sciences—Permanence of Paper for Printed Library Materials Z39.48-1992 (R1997).

To The Truth That Sets Us Free

If we could only remember—in the Now—the fact that there
always come to us those telling moments when nothing
that mattered before matters as it once did, when the
things formerly prized are seen as being virtually without
value to us, *then* . . .

Perhaps we might know our lives painted upon a broader
canvas . . . where our days would not be filled with their
shallow strokes of petty self-concerns, but with the
gentle brush of what is True and Timeless.

And should we—for the sake of being present to ourselves in
the Now —be able to see within ourselves this broad new
scale of Being, then we would also *know* that Life itself
has never weighed in upon us so heavily as to hurt us,
rather . . .

It was we who, in ignorance of Reality, carelessly attributed
weight to events that were without substance, causing
ourselves to fear and suffer nothing less than the fervent
magnitude of our own imagination.

Contents

Foreword

Human beings can always use more Light.

It's not that there isn't plenty to be had; the Light of conscious revelation pours down unendingly. The problem is that most of us have blocked ourselves from receiving genuine healing Light by focusing our attention on the false light of self-centered thought. And it isn't just individuals who suffer because of this. The sad state of affairs we see in the larger world today reflects the growing isolation of men and women who have cut themselves off from real life through misplaced attention.

But isolation is not a necessary outcome. We can learn to look beyond the limited world that our thoughts present to us and come into direct contact with reality itself. The goal of all truthful teachings handed down through the ages has been to encourage individuals to follow the path to a more expansive existence. We're told to wake up; to shake off the illusion that our thoughts about ourselves, and life, are all there is; and to put ahead of our own ideas of what we need the wishes of something that's greater than we are. If we take the bold step of sacrificing our *thoughts about life* in favor of a *real life*, we will be given everything in return: security, love, wisdom, and all the benefits of a fearless life.

For close to thirty years, Guy Finley has been sharing this message of Light with men and women from around the world and all walks of life, revealing both the foundation of our problems within our own undeveloped selves and the process through which we can grow and enter into a new relationship with life that is the essence of genuine fulfillment. In Guy's writings and in his talks, he has looked at the subject from every angle, showing ever new facets of the priceless gem that is the Truth.

The body of Guy's work is extensive, and part of what makes *The Essential Laws of Fearless Living* shine is that it draws from this vast resource of aphorisms, insights, and special writings. The central theme of the book is that our thoughts lead us into illusion, and then we are misled into interacting with those illusions instead of with real life. The result is all manner of limitation: limitation in what we think we can do, limitation in what we believe and hope the world will provide us, limitation in relationships—essentially, limitation in every aspect of our moment-to-moment experience.

And there's an even more subtle, soul-undermining effect that comes of living in illusion: it puts us into an antagonistic relationship with life as it unfolds. Whenever reality threatens an illusion—which it does most of the time—we take it as a personal assault. Rarely do things go exactly as we want and believe we need. Everywhere, people and events conspire to frustrate us and take away even the little we have—or so it seems. The "natural" response is anger, fear, depression, and a sense of having been betrayed.

But negativity is not the only possibility for us. I once heard Guy say something simply stunning that could almost serve as a key lesson for this entire book. He said, *"The perfected human being is the one who only sees perfection."*

Every moment *is* perfect because it brings us exactly what we need to be able to see through an illusion that keeps us in pain; it gives us the opportunity to break through that limitation by entering into full awareness. In each chapter of *The Essential Laws of Fearless Living,* Guy shows us that everything that happens to us is a gift. It provides the next step in the process of our perfection—if we will only see it as such. This truly is the solution to every heartache, and if you meet this book actively, with a willingness to learn its lessons, it can heal your life.

It doesn't matter if you're a longtime student of the principles Guy Finley presents, or this is your first introduction to his writings; *The Essential Laws of Fearless Living* provides a wonderful opportunity to dip into the work of a modern-day master and find inspiration and enlightenment in this extensive collection of specially selected nuggets of truth. As in all his works, Guy addresses deep matters—the secrets of the universe itself—and he does so in a way that makes this important material fascinating, compelling, and filled with the sense that great mysteries are being revealed. Above all, he makes the truth *useable,* so that you can make these principles the cornerstone of your daily experience.

Whether in any moment you want simply to bask in a quick ray of sunshine, or you decide to linger a while to follow the path that ray illuminates and delve deeper into the subject, this book fills that need. Enjoy this rich assortment of higher principles, and may it bring much Light into your life.

Dr. Ellen Dickstein

In Gratitude

To VH, K, BR, G, JC, O, MN, RC, B, CA, MO

Thanks to all who have gone before me ... to reveal the Way; thanks to those who have stood by me ... along the Way; and thanks to those who have opposed me ... along the Way. Your individual efforts are, and continue to be, invaluable and inseparable from the works of mine that they have helped to birth.

And deepest thanks of all to my wife, Patricia ... who never fails to help me see and understand that all that really matters in life is love.

Author's Word

This book offers the reader something more than any other work of mine has yet to do: carefully woven into this book's forty-one individual chapter sections are fourteen special essays from selected works of mine.

Five of these fourteen entries are new writings comprised from a few of my latest audio albums, including *The Secret of Being Unstoppable, Seven Steps to Oneness*, and *The Meditative Life*. These essays offer the reader the opportunity to explore works of mine that have never before been published in this kind of format.

The remaining nine essays (in this mini-anthology) are carefully adapted from six of my most popular books, including *The Secret of Letting Go, Design Your Destiny*, and *Let Go and Live in the Now*. And, just in case you've read one (or some) of my past works, please know this: in all cases special care was taken to rewrite these selected sections in order to serve and support the central theme of this newest work on fearless living.

Each chapter of this new book is presented in step-by-step sections designed to gently lead the reader into higher and higher levels of self-understanding. And, at the end of each chapter, there are special Key Lessons in Review. These short but powerful summaries of the main chapter ideas are special insights intended to help you actualize the new principles just presented.

Persist with your wish to be free. Nothing in the universe can stand in your way; all that is right, bright, and true stands behind you!

Chapter 1

WELCOME THE LIGHT THAT MAKES LIFE BRIGHT

Let Go and Grow Beyond the Limitation of Illusions

KEY LESSON

The true depth and breadth of the heart is measured not
only by what it can hold, but also by how willing it is to let go.

There is no brighter gift, no greater potential given to us human beings, than the presence of a timeless Light within us whose power makes all things possible. Its celestial character knows we have not been created to live as the captives of *any* fearful condition, let alone those we unconsciously create for ourselves.

This ever-quiet, always present Light goes before us at all times, as illumination of a lamp moves ahead of the one who walks by the safety of its beams. This little metaphor helps explain many things. For instance, one wonders, If this Light is *already* within us—a timeless power whose presence makes things right—then why do we run into as many problems as we do? With such a source of courage at the very center of us, why do our fears outpace our ability to put them behind us? As we are about to see, the answer to both these questions is amazingly simple.

What good is the light of any lamp in the dark *if we forget to take that lamp with us* out into the night? In other words, what good is this fearless nature of ours if we can't remember that to walk through life without our Light means we are likely to stumble and "fall into a pit"? Together we will find the answer to this important question, along with much, much more. As we uncover the cause of why we forget our True Self, we also recover its native fearlessness ... all in one clean action. Soon comes a whole new way to live, laugh, and love.

Over the course of our studies, we will examine the secretive nature of this indwelling Light, looking at it from many different angles. It has almost as many names as there are tongues to speak it; but, in the end, regardless of what one calls it—God, True Self, Christ, Krishna, Atman, one's Higher Power, Buddha nature—it is still one voice, calling for a singular action. So if any of these names disturb you, just drop them; in and of themselves, they are of no real importance.

We could just as easily think of this Divine character as our own sleeping conscience: the part of ourselves that knows—*without having to think about it*—what is right from what is wrong, true from false. It is that "still small voice" within us that is incapable of compromising itself and that would rather perish than cause unnecessary pain to another. This celestial part of our individual consciousness *lives in everyone,* and even though we humans number in the billions, our conscience is one. By its Light we are empowered to see things as they are; through its encompassing intelligence we understand, at once, the beautiful wholeness of things and their many separate relationships. And as the Light of this new awareness dawns within us, we become the very things we have sought for and fought for all of our lives: compassion, wisdom, kindness, courage, and love.

Our spiritual task, assuming we are stirred to seek this truth of ourselves, is to awaken ourselves to this Light that first invites us and then unites us with its uncompromised life. Our receptivity to its abiding presence is our connectivity to its fearlessness, and accordingly we are empowered to possess ourselves; for as we enter into its life we not only see what is right, bright, and timeless, but we also come to realize these beautiful qualities as being one and the same as our True Self.

Nor does it matter if we "believe" or not in the powers of this living Light that is discussed in the pages that follow. Belief is a hand-me-down, a poor substitute for direct relationship with the veracities that are one with our own higher consciousness. "When you believe in things that you don't understand, then you suffer; superstition ain't the way," writes songwriter Stevie Wonder. Together we shall prove the existence of a Light whose timeless life and love is self-evident. As we learn the wisdom of welcoming it into our lives, we will earn the fearless life for which our heart of hearts longs.

What does matter—and is the whole purpose of this book—is our individual awakening to this most indwelling Light. Our hope is nothing less than to realize conscious relationship with its Life; for then ours will be—without stress or strain—*the effortless awareness of what is our own, and what is not our own.* Now, should you be wondering what the value is of such a seemingly innocent power, here's the surprising answer—in depth. When all is said and done, what is it that we suffer over other than finding out that something we thought belonged to us ... doesn't! You name it: persons, powers, praise, possessions ... even our own life proves itself not our own in the appointed time.

Before we can hope to let go of all that is not our own—with all of the painful relationships attending these mistaken conclusions—we must be able to see them as such, beginning with this revelation: No fearful sense of limitation or inadequacy belongs to our True Self. As we awaken to see this truth, by the Light of what is real within us, we also make this most astonishing discovery: We already have everything we need to succeed. Let's pause here for a moment and see how this realization changes our reality.

As we realize that our compulsive need to control life is no longer necessary, or that we don't have to have someone or something in our life to lend us a sense of being whole, we gradually stop resisting the changing conditions around us that once threatened these *imagined* needs. Which means we are released from all forms of feeling ourselves inadequate to these false tasks of trying to fulfill ourselves. Now, instead of fearing unexpected changes, we have a new "role" in life: we are a consciously grateful participant in its ceaseless unfolding. How nice.

A big part of learning to welcome this Light that liberates us from our fears requires that we do the interior work of seeing where we have been living from false conclusions: mistaken ideas about life and ourselves that we believed to be real but that are not. As we have already seen, it isn't until we see the truth of our condition that we stop participating in our own punishment. The world becomes a better place for us, because we stop wasting everything in it in order to free ourselves from things that are illusions in the first place.

Let's see for ourselves where we have reached some of these self-compromising conclusions that are supported by unsuspected illusions.

One common illusion is that *the world revealed to us through our senses is the whole of reality.* In other words, our present nature believes that everything worthwhile—that is, pleasurable—has to do with what we can extract from our relationships, business, money, powers, and so on. We look into this world that we see as being outside of us, hoping to find something in it to complete us. What we don't see is that the nature that searches the world outside of itself—to make itself feel whole and real—has set itself apart from that which it hopes will heal it. It divides to conquer; but this level of self can never overcome the unhappiness that is born of its own divided state!

The "healing" we need, the sense of wholeness for which we search, has nothing to do with adding anything to ourselves. This needed healing comes from recognizing that the pain we have—along with the suffering inherent in being negative over this pain—is born out of participating in a series of illusions that have been handed down from generation to generation!

Who in their right mind would educate anyone—let alone their children—that the answer to heartache is to further stress oneself by struggling to control conditions outside of ourselves? The only thing we "win" for such effort is to become the inadvertent slave of what we hoped would free us. Or what about trying to distract ourselves from what "dogs" us in life—as if running toward a pleasure changes the fact that something is barking at our heels, making us run from its unwanted presence?

We are divided within, serving two masters that are secretly one. There's what we *don't* want—our deep-seated desire to avoid anything seen as being unpleasant—and then there's its other half: an equally strong desire that presses us to find a suitable substitute for whatever life seems to refuse us in the moment. Our identification with this divided self keeps us from knowing the peace of mind and fullness of heart that is being whole in the here and now. So this is the first illusion, and the first and last lesson in true self-liberation: the real world *is not* what our thoughts and feelings would have us believe it is.

We must begin the necessary work of welcoming the Light that leads to letting go; our soul task is to release ourselves from an unconscious relationship with a false self whose imagined conclusions—about how to find lasting peace—are the secret source of conflict on this planet. Then, liberated by the Light of understanding, we will enter and know—as our own—a brand new world in which happiness and wholeness are one and the same.

Adapted in part from the audio
album *The Illusion of Limitation*

New Rules to Rise Above Whatever Is in Your Way

KEY LESSON

The main reason we must always remember to hold our chin up whenever negative thoughts try to drag us down is that whichever direction we choose first, in that moment, is the one the rest of us will follow.

Rebecca had decided that her best chance of getting hired by a company doing geological survey work in the Alaskan wilderness was to earn a private license to fly twin-engine planes. A few days later she began taking lessons from a wise old bush pilot, highly respected throughout the region for his cool and collected ways of dealing with the worst possible situations.

After the mandatory ground schooling, at which Rebecca excelled, and during her fourth lesson in the sky, the flight instructor gave her what she thought was a special treat: Taking his hands off the yoke, he turned the flight controls over to her. There she was, just as she had dreamed, sitting tall in the copilot's seat with the flight stick firmly in her hands.

Rebecca felt as though she was literally on "cloud 9"—at least, until a scant moment later when she found herself rudely awakened from her dream. She tried shaking her head to get rid of what was before her eyes, but that did not work. In the distance, through the windshield, she could see something rushing toward her faster than what she could think to do about it!

Right in the path of the plane, and seeming to have appeared out of nowhere, a huge snow-capped mountain lay dead ahead. Transfixed by its sheer mass, Rebecca found herself as frozen at the stick as were the iced and craggy peaks stretched out before her. And she was headed straight for them! A deep chill came into the cabin.

All along the wise old instructor was watching her closely, studying her reactions. Of course, she didn't know it, but he had turned the controls over to her for just this test now taking place. He waited until the last moment he could, and was just about to take over again, when Rebecca snapped out of her fear-induced trance. She looked away from the mountain and turned to face him.

Then, in a voice so trembling and timid that it even scared her, she broke the tense silence of the moment. "Sir," she said, "please take over the controls. I'm afraid we are about to crash!" His reply stunned her. "No," he spoke quietly, "I don't think I will. After all, it's your flight."

It was getting harder for her to take in a whole breath, as if she were standing in the oxygen-thin air atop the great white mountain before them. Struggling to control her voice, she dug down into herself and managed to ask one more question of her teacher: "Then what should I do? Please, tell me what to do!"

She looked over at him again, and was surprised to see virtually no worry at all upon his face. His calm demeanor helped to steady her nerves. She took a deep breath and relaxed her hands that had just about choked the life out of the control yoke. The next moment he gave her a short three-word instruction, and she knew everything would soon be all right. He simply said, "Change your altitude."

"Of course," her own mind echoed back to his command, and a split second later she pulled firmly back on the yoke; the craft responded by rising, and mere moments later the icy peak passed beneath her and out of sight.

As Rebecca sat there, relieved by the results of her actions, she was struck by two things at once: How could she have forgotten that the controls were in her hands, and at least as important, why had she been unable to remember this on her own? At that moment, soaring at ten thousand feet above the ground, she made a silent vow never again to forget the lesson of this day: *She could choose her own altitude.*

Doesn't this short truth tale remind you of a certain kind of spiritual strength that you know belongs to you but that you have somehow forgotten or misplaced? It ought to; after all, how many of us look out ahead of ourselves at some unwanted event that looms too large and find ourselves feeling out of control ... headed for what seems an unavoidable collision?

Wouldn't it be nice to be able to reach down inside of ourselves, grab hold of the controls of our own consciousness, and pull ourselves up? To quietly watch that would-be mountain of a problem, whatever it is, pass by harmlessly below us, even as we reach ever-higher and happier skies?

We can learn to do this. Such a power is not just a pipe dream; ours is the ability to take conscious control of our spiritual altitude. But this greatest of gifts is given to us only in proportion to our willingness to awaken from those unconscious parts of ourselves that not only become transfixed before challenging events but are the secret creators of the very things into which we crash! This is why we must work in every moment to remain inwardly awake—to be aware of our attitude toward our life as it unfolds before and around us: so that whenever we find a negative attitude in ourselves—some form of dark thought or feeling trying to drag us down—we don't say "I" to it. In a manner of speaking, we pull up and away from that part of ourselves by withdrawing our consent to be confined by how it would define us. This kind of conscious action on our part changes not only what we perceive as being possible in the moment, but it also empowers us—in the same moment—to see and make new and higher choices.

Seen or not, our attitude determines our altitude in life. The "low" life comes by default. Gravity guarantees we will reach the bottom. To go higher begins with *choosing to be* higher. Realizing that the power to leave dark states beneath and behind us begins with recognizing that who we really are—our True Nature—has as much in common with self-limiting thoughts and feelings as does the open sky with the crow that wings through it!

Remember this one great lesson: Do the moment-to-moment work of dropping anything that wants to drag you down, and Truth itself will see to it that you rise.

Find New Strength in Awakened Attention

KEY LESSON

Whether for its joy or sorrow, whatever we wish for
another person comes true for us in the same moment we
make that wish!

Imagine for a moment a woman who inherits an antique jewelry box from a loving grandparent. She puts the cherished keepsake on her makeup bureau, next to her own collection of mostly costume jewelry, but never really pays it much mind. And there it sits. But what she doesn't know is that her grandmother hid a priceless diamond ring within it, in a secret compartment. It's hers to have, if only she knew where to look for it. But will she?

In many ways this is a story not unlike our own: for "hidden" within each of us, and yet in plain sight, is a power unmatched in its brilliance. What is this potential diamond of the mind that awaits whoever will find it? It is our ability to *attend* to what we will. Coupled with awareness, attention empowers us to unite ourselves with whatever we wish to know and be. Let's examine this largely unexplored gift of ours.

Much as we just learned in the preceding section—that we have the right to remember what we choose to—so are we graced with an immense interior gift: the power to give our attention to what we will—to what enriches and serves us.

Continuing states of stress and sorrow are the result of having mistakenly placed our attention upon what punishes us, stealing from us our happiness as a result. The following new self-knowledge reveals the secret ins and outs of this dark dynamic: Any time our attention is given to some thought or feeling, it animates that condition; our attention invests what it falls on with a certain kind of life energy. Another unknown phenomenon about attention is that when it is given to something—for instance, a timeless night sky—it facilitates within us a union with the qualities of that "world." And this dynamic is in operation all the time: to consider something is to be connected to it. So, our attention connects, animates, and nourishes whatever we lend it to in life. And more than this, but as a part of its power, we have all witnessed the following:

You're stopped at a red light, and you look out your car window at someone passing by. You follow him with your eyes—interested in something about his appearance or manner. As you remotely study this person, the power of attention moves through and across time and space and it "touches" him in some way. The next thing you know he turns around and looks at you!

This power can be used for good or bad. When we use it for practical work, or for honest self-observation, we use it to our own benefit. However, when this power operates on its own, within us, *without our awareness of what it's interacting with,* it can cause many problems. Here is where the unattended mind becomes the breeding ground of self-defeat. For instance, any time our attention is placed, without our knowing it, on some way to escape ourselves, here's what happens: more often than not we find out—too late—we got hooked up with some self-harming idea that ultimately led us to compromise ourselves.

This new kind of self-knowledge places us on the threshold of a wholly different, brighter life. If by being inattentive to our own interior life, we see how much of our unhappiness is self-created, then, we can learn to reclaim and redirect our attention, placing it within what is right and bright. But, there is only one way to realize this reversal: we must work to see how wrongly directed attention works against us.

Perhaps a thought pops into your mind about a problem that's been bothering you. Appearing with it is some emotional disturbance. Now the thought starts rolling, growing in its demand for your attention. Almost instantly it has defined what needs to be done, or what you are powerless to do. And both states accomplish the same dark end: You've unknowingly animated that thought and given it a life—and the life you've given it is your own! Here's an example of how this scene might unfold:

A man is walking through his office when his boss walks by and gives him a blank look. The thought pops into the man's mind that his boss is criticizing him or doesn't like him. Now, as he starts to fear this idea—a negative picture produced by his imagination—his mind focuses its attention on this disturbing image. And the more he attends to this dark dream, the further into its labyrinth he descends, strengthening its presence and power to further irritate him. A heartbeat later, he has no doubt: the boss has it in for him! This thought grows in authority for him, tormenting him for the rest of the day and causing him to snap at his family when he gets home. And all of this suffering is born of what? The conjunction of a passing glance and a moment of misdirected attention!

Here's the amazing thing about this illustration, and what we want to learn from it: this whole drama has been played out inside of the man—storyline, stage, cast, and leading characters.

But he doesn't see how this painful state is self-created; instead he believes it has been cast upon him by someone else—his heartless boss! So, what else can he do—being in the dark as he is to his true condition—but try to rid himself of his stressed feelings? How? By arguing with his boss, either outwardly or in his mind. The more he feels punished by the situation *that he sees in his mind,* the more he wants to fight with it. He's sure his unwanted experience exists independent of his perception of it, but we can see he's mistaken. His pain is a product of how he sees the event and then all of the misery that comes with resisting his own mistaken perception. He is quite literally lashing himself, and the more he resists what he thinks is happening, the more it happens to him! This is a good description of what I call the "circle of self." In it we can see how the pain of our own mistaken perception produces the enemies it needs to keep itself alive.

From our vantage point, we can see how the man's unattended mind first animated a fearful thought, which leads to wrongly feeding it with his own life. We can also see that nothing can change for him until he sees the truth behind his trouble and withdraws his consent from it.

We suffer because we consort with painful thoughts and feelings, thinking somehow that not wanting them makes them go away. But our unconscious actions betray us: first, by animating what makes us ache, and then by binding us to that relationship through our resistance to it. Here's a simple way of saying these last few ideas: *Not wanting our negative states actually nourishes them!* I can almost hear the question that comes next: "Wait a minute! You can't be saying these dark thoughts and feelings are good, and that we should want what's hurting us, are you?"

Of course not! Negative states have no right to exist in us as they presently do. And that's just the point. We literally give them a place to live in our psychic system—feed them, as it were—by trying to rid ourselves of them in the usual ways. But there are other ways of dealing with pervasive dark states besides resisting them, suppressing them, or trying to change the conditions seen as being responsible for them. *Instead of these acts of willfulness, we choose in favor of watchfulness.* Rather than struggling with dark states, learning to be quietly watchful of them does two things at once: first, it separates us from being wrongly identified with our own thoughts about that troublesome state. Second—by the light of our newly liberated attention—we catch a glimpse of a powerful insight whose light helps set us free:

If we mistakenly give any negative state its "life"—then the opposite must hold true: we can consciously withdraw that same life any time we so choose!

Here is a simple exercise to help you get started with this new kind of seeing that is the power behind freeing you. Several times each day, whenever you can remember to do it, deliberately disconnect yourself from your own thinking. Choose awareness of your thoughts over being absorbed in the sensations they produce as they carry you along to get what they want. The aim here is simple: reclaim your attention in order *to be where you are,* and then just quietly notice all that you can about yourself. The light of this new order of awareness empowers you to catch and release what your own unattended thoughts had been busy cooking up for you, using you as stock!

Each time you remember to reclaim your attention in this manner, with it you regain your life. And here is a bright bit of encouragement to help you get started. The words that follow are those of Simone Weil, a brilliant French writer, activist, and lover of the Light: "Even if our efforts of attention seem for years to be producing no result, one day a light that is in exact proportion to them will flood the soul."

Adapted in part from
Who Put That Stone in My Shoe?

Stand on the Unshakable Ground of Your True Self

KEY LESSON

Seen properly, what is any dark mental or emotional habit—such as fearfully trying to protect ourselves from what "may be"—other than the unconscious practice of perfecting what punishes us?

Here is a particularly vital idea for those of us who are tired of finding ourselves a surprised victim of our own actions: in this world of ours, *response is request*. We can slightly enlarge this idea by restating it this way: The way you respond to life is also a request you make to it. See how the next example proves this important discovery.

Someone walks into your home or office and says something that just steams you. Instantly you see "red," and then you sit and simmer over what's taken place long after the offending party has left. But here's what you don't see: your continuing negative state—your response to the event—acts as a request to all those you encounter in the hours to come. It's a law: people tend to treat us as they find us treating ourselves, and when we meet them with some kind of misery, they reflect the same back to us. Surely we've all seen how "like attracts like." In this context it should be clear: *Our refusal to let go of some negative state amounts to a request for its continuity.*

Whenever I present ideas like these to groups, invariably someone will get upset and say something like, "You're wrong! I don't want to feel as I do, and I certainly don't agree to be taken over by some dark feeling. The truth is there are times when negativity just overcomes me, regardless of what I wish."

Of course this happens, just as you've described—which is the point, really: No one is saying that each of us isn't doing the very best we can at the moment. Believe it or not, even common criminals are doing the best they can right in the commission of that crime that will one day lock them away. In scale, haven't we found ourselves captives of some choice that we thought would set us free? Too late we learned that what "burned" us was our own best idea! The point is this: We can only do what we know to do, and if we want to do better, we must learn something better to do—such as follows.

Most of us have found ourselves washed away, overcome by a flood of punishing thoughts and feelings. Picture a desperate man being swept down a river, grabbing onto whatever comes along, and it's easy to see how we end up clinging to things that—rather than saving us—actually serve to further sink us. "From the frying pan into the fire" is the expression that defines "bad bounce" relationships, addictions, and a host of other self-compromising acts meant to end one's misery, not extend it.

There is only one reason any pain has the power to command us as it does. We have forgotten this one great rescuing truth: *No dark state has authority over who we really are!* This is spiritual fact, pure and simple; but why can't we remember it in our hour of need?

The answer is somewhat shocking: in those moments when the Light that lives within us is meant to transform whatever troubles us into a new and higher form of self-understanding, *it is we who get transformed into that trouble itself!* Here's a look at how we get so turned around: we become the very negative state we don't want by *identifying with* our resistance to it. And we all know what happens next. It is no longer we who meet life, who welcome the lessons it brings; instead the conflict we are in goes before us, as do dark clouds before the storm. Seen in this light, it's little wonder that we receive what we do back from life. After all, what do lightning rods attract?

Every one of us knows—from somewhere deep in the heart of us—that we were not created to spend our lives contesting whatever dominates us in the moment. And yet, we can see how each unwanted state that washes over us is replaced by another state of some similar ilk. It's pretty clear: we're never truly in possession of ourselves, unless we believe that not wanting to be unhappy or anxious is the same as being calm and content. Our sense of self is on a kind of "spin cycle" running through a series of alternating states where, for example, resentment washes over us until it's replaced by some form of guilt or regret; then guilt is washed away by a feeling of trying to find or give forgiveness. And we feel better until another cycle starts … again. So now we must ask ourselves, "How can any order of consciousness that continuously repeats itself request anything genuinely new from life?"

The answer is clear. It can't; which means we must abandon all hope in our usual way of responding to what challenges us. What's needed is a whole new way to ask life for what we really want—to live from an unshakable self that cannot be made to act against itself or anyone else. This is where new and true self-knowledge is irreplaceable, as is about to be made self-evident.

Your True Nature is something already greater than any self-compromising state, much in the same way as the ocean shoreline is greater than the waves that pound it. Your True Self is the unshakable Ground over which all "waves" of thoughts and feelings both move and break. And just as light doesn't fight with shadows for fear of what the shadows portend, neither need we ever do anything about our interior troubles except meet them from this timeless Ground within us. This willingness to be inwardly still and take no action toward our interior troubles is one and the same as our new request. How so? Deliberate *non-action* toward whatever threatens to wash us away is the same as asking our God to lift us above these troublesome waves.

The beauty of making this new kind of conscious request is that the rescuing response to it is immediate—only in ways formerly unimaginable to us! Here's just a hint of what we see each time we "choose the higher Ground" instead of habitually identifying with negative thoughts and feelings.

We realize these various mental and emotional states are *visitors,* not who we are. We see that while negative states are within us, they are not our True Nature any more than superheated deep sea vents are the same as the waters they warm. And by our choice to remain aware of their presence within us—instead of identifying with the pain they bring—we are instantly "transported" to that higher Ground within us: a higher state of our present self that dwells worlds above the waves that used to sink us. Only then and there is the real difference evident between Self and its states, just as a man standing on the beach knows the difference between sand and sea.

Practice this new interior understanding that starts with remembering the truth of yourself. Each effort will reward you with the growing realization that any time you start to feel miserable it's only because you have mistakenly identified with *who and what you are not*. Learn what it means to seek out and stand on the unshakable Ground of True Self. Be one with who you really are, and the waves of a thousand passing worlds cannot wash you away.

Adapted in part from *The Lost Secrets of Prayer*

1. The main reason to hold our chin up whenever some negative thought tries to drag us down is that whichever direction we choose in that moment is the one we will follow. As goes our attention, so comes our experience.

2. To flee the fight, or be the Light, that is the question!

3. Knowledge without Spirit is like finding yourself on a cold night with all the wood in the world and not a flame with which to light it.

4. If you will do what you are doing in the moment, you cannot undo yourself.

5. One thing that makes negative states so difficult to drop is the illusion they create within us that no choice exists other than to cave in to their punishing presence. But, in truth, it is not we who are without choice in such moments: it is the negative state that has no choice but to disappear once we remember that no darkness is greater than the Light.

Chapter 2

BUILD THE FOUNDATION
OF A FEARLESS LIFE

New Self-Understanding That
Makes You Unstoppable

KEY LESSON

We must do the work to prove our fears groundless; otherwise it is our fears that will gain ground and our lives will be spent in their service.

Have you ever wondered if other people see things in the same way that you do? For instance, though it has gone on for decades, there has been a recent rash of over-the-top white-collar crime. It would seem that having multimillions isn't enough for some folks, so they steal money from their own companies, leaving employees out in the cold. Now, couple this blatant criminal behavior with the following curious fact: Many of these wildly successful executives admit they are haunted by a daily fear of failure. Now what seems obvious (to me)—and yet no one seems to see—is this: Our present-day definition of success makes no sense at all! What sane person would envy living in the kind of environment in which insatiable greed and fear are always prowling around in the back of one's mind?

So, either our whole notion of what it means to succeed is mistaken or—as is in fact the case—over time we have become identified with a wrong idea about what it means to be a "winner." Following is the true meaning of a successful life. Please read it at least twice so that something of its subtle nature has the chance to stir your mind:

Real success is a creative state of being that comes with living in conscious relationship with an Intelligence that never fears

---

Now, with this new idea fresh in our minds, let's examine the
difference between the kind of "success" whose fruit is a fearful
life and that fearless Life that is success itself. Then we'll look at
what we need to know to realize within ourselves that greater
estate in which fear can't dwell.

For most of us, the recipe for success remains much the same
as it has been for generations before us. Pursue the dream. Pay
the price. And then hope to possess those powers we imagine
come with the package we just bought: a lasting sense of security coupled with continual contentment.

In other words, go out into the world and take from it what
we need in order to feel fearless. But here's the "catch"—and
why no one wins peace of mind with what they find at the end
of these rainbows. This kind of success, both in terms of what
we hope to win as well as the "powers" it promises to grant us,
is an illusion.

Yes, we can come to own the object we desire—yes, we can
win the position we see as being the path to "power"—but
here's why we can never hope to possess *ourselves* through these
achievements alone: our newly won sense of strength and security—its fearlessness—is as fleeting as are those conditions we
are now dependent upon in order to sustain our imagined sense
of self!

Experience proves this finding: Our usual efforts to enrich
ourselves do not grant us the independence we fight to win;
instead we find ourselves increasingly dependent, captives of an
ever-escalating struggle to keep our imagined security in place.

We have not risen above what compromises us; we have unconsciously fueled it, and, in the end, we don't so much find ourselves returned to a life filled with familiar fears as we see that we have never left it.

Let's summarize our discoveries so far: The more we imagine a fearless life created by conditions outside of us, the more compelled we feel to try and control those same conditions. Our fear is that any change in those conditions will return us back to where we started: searching for a way to be fearless. Yet, the more we resist change, the more afraid we become of it. We find ourselves applying more and more pressure to life in order to escape the mounting pressure born of our own demands. And gradually, instead of being a vital human being—receptive and naturally responsive to any and all life-altering impressions—we become static and psychological "shut-ins," captives of our own aversion to a fear we unconsciously create.

We do not have to remain the victims of this dark and downward-trending circle of self. The truth is there is no real reason at all to resist the world as it turns. In fact, rather than fearing what cannot be foreseen, one day you will be grateful for it, and here's why: we are not just created to go through constant change, our True Self is the changing ground of life itself. From out of its unfathomable depths pour the unseen forces that design, drive, and ultimately perfect the transformation of consciousness. Can we see how the realization of such a truth about our own higher Self would have to spell the end of fear? Good! Then let's gather the light we'll need to actualize that new freedom!

Three of the most powerful words in the English language are *I can learn*. We are, of course, speaking in terms of our spiritual life, although the same truth applies across the board in all human endeavors. We *can* learn how to get what we want from this world. But, to the point of this study, we are created with the ability to do much more than just manifest the things we desire. Living within us is all the illumination we need to dismiss any dark fear created by our own unbridled desires.

As we are coming to see, within each of us dwells a Light—an awareness capable not only of observing the host of invisible forces that forge life itself, but whose conscious interaction with them changes them as *it will*. It is through this higher order of ourselves that we are empowered to learn the truth about ourselves. And here the word *truth* means not just intellectual self-knowledge, but a direct in-dwelling *knowing* of all that is for our further perfection and all that seems to oppose it. This beautiful understanding, once awakened within us, transforms the way we see life. There is no longer any reason to fear "how" things change because we're beginning to understand the greatest secret on Earth:

Our True Self is the stage, its actors, and the director of everything that changes anywhere!

Consider for a moment the meaning of this insight.

If you were empowered to change life—in order to give yourself whatever is always good and true for you to know and have—would you *ever* make any other kind of changes? For example, would you fear unexpected events, such as a loss of some kind? No! Even though they may come as a surprise, *you already know* that they herald a new beginning of something better.

Would you resist the passage of time and the slow changes that grow out of it like branches on a tree? No! *You already know* that patience and willingness to persist through what is being revealed—even if momentarily bitter—will bring only sweeter fruits.

Would you resent those moments when a door closes on some anticipated pleasure? No! *You already know* that such "problems" are actually secret passageways waiting to reveal themselves if you'll watch for their eventual opening. Mountains crumble in the presence of the person who knows how to wait for a passage through them. Real power, real fearlessness, is knowing that there's only one reason life changes as it does: *It is to reveal the secret Goodness underlying those same changes.*

Aren't the changing seasons themselves evidence of a reality always in transition yet ever serving to perfect the world through which they pass? If we know how to look, all around us is the proof of an active Intelligence that is greater than what it acts upon. *So does this hold true within us?* Yes, we live in a world of changes; but within it, within us, exists something that—for its timeless nature knows that the changes taking place are merely momentary reflections of a broader and unchanging life.

It is this understanding that helps us to let go of whatever we insist upon—with all the fear that attends such demands—and that allows us to wait on the Light of God to show us safe passage through the changes we face. Our quiet willingness to remain watchful in this way—instead of being willful—reveals and proves in us a new kind of unstoppable power: a Light that fears nothing because it is part of a celestial Intelligence that never stops changing and that, in turn, never stops transforming any world within which its Light is present.

Practically speaking, as our fear diminishes, our confidence increases; we grow in patience; a true optimism about life pervades everything we do, even when we run into obstacles. For us, it isn't a question of whether things will work out in our favor; our only wonder is when that gift will present itself. We stop running; we know now there is nowhere we have to get to—and that there is nothing for us to get away from. *We are the life we want*, and the Life we are is without fear because it is one with the Light.

Adapted in part from the audio
album *Secrets of Being Unstoppable*

Be Your True Self and Be Fearless

KEY LESSON

The imitation of greatness gives rise to fear, but when
we will dare to be ourselves—in spite of the fears—we
awaken within us the character of that Greatness we long
to know.

We can either spend our lives fearful of any unwanted event that comes along that might challenge our sense of self—or we can use that same situation to help set ourselves free. Presently we see whatever troubles us through the eyes of a false nature that believes protecting itself from what it fears is the same as being fearless. The only way this idea makes sense is if we think that avoiding a problem means we've overcome it. What other way is there of dealing with what frightens us if all forms of resistance are futile? Here's the one true solution: It is possible for us to know so much about the nature of fear that, one day, it simply runs out of ways to make us believe in its shaking.

The following three insights are designed to help us look at our old, familiar fearful reactions in a whole new way. But taken altogether, these key ideas tell the story of a whole new kind of self-understanding powerful enough to penetrate fear's protective shell—dispelling both the feared and the fearful at once. The Light that remains is freedom.

1. Self-awakening, and the new order of freedom that attends it, begins within seeing through what is not real, just as freedom from the terror of a nightmare begins with discovering you've been asleep, having a bad dream.

2. No fact is frightening unless it runs into conflict with what we want. When this happens, the fear is not in the event, but in us—we who have decided that in order to feel secure, life must jump through our hoop. So, the fear we feel is in our hoop, not the fact that life has jumped unexpectedly.

3. It is in our power to discover that who we really are has nothing to fear, but that we make ourselves fearful each time we look outside of ourselves for some power to make us feel fearless.

Why is it that we will challenge and then work to change the world's opinions as they concern us, but we never question our own beliefs no matter how much fear-filled stress and anxiety they produce within us?

For example, we wouldn't dream of diving for sunken treasure in our bathtub because we know that the best we can hope to find there are a few plastic pearls. Yet we still dive headlong into this world every day, hoping to prove ourselves as someone "special." And we do this in spite of the fact that, to date, our struggles have failed to provide us with anything more than just another temporary identity as fearful as our former one. But here's another fact, a much brighter one. It explains why our lives don't have to remain as they have been: It isn't an unyielding world that withholds from us what we need to be happy, whole, and quietly confident. The only thing making us fearful and discontented is our belief in the altogether wrong idea that our value in life depends upon others agreeing to it!

What is it that feeds this belief—that drives this insatiable desire to become "someone" in this world of ours? In a word, the wish for *power*. With it, we believe we are elevated above a crushing world of others who want at all costs what we want— to end their struggle with fear. Without it, we feel not only unprotected, but unremarkable: our daily affairs seem to have little to no meaning because we're sure no one recognizes our worth. And while most of us would deny we live from this kind of self-enclosed mindset, the evidence of our continuing fear proves we live from its bitter conclusion. If we would be free, then what we need is the light of a new understanding about "how" this unconscious conviction keeps us its captive.

Neatly hidden within this false belief in the "power of being someone"—not unlike the tempting poison apple offered to Snow White by the evil queen—is the opposite of this belief, which looks something like this: the failure to become someone in our own eyes—or in the eyes of others—means we will be powerless in life! Without such power we can wave good-bye to our hope for permanent security and its happiness; it will evaporate and vanish, taking with it our chance to be free.

It is *this* unconscious and unchallenged conclusion that drives men and women to the point of collapse. Clearly this force that compels us is not just the desire to attain some imagined pleasure; we run as we do to escape the threat of unceasing discontentment. Let's put it this way: We have not been running to something—that goal or that dream—as much as we have been running from the fear of being no one.

This is a race that we can never hope to win, because we are tied to whatever we avoid. It's a law: What we resist persists, and this also explains why, so far, fear has set the course and the pace of our race through life. What needs to be done is clear: We must do the work to prove our fears groundless, otherwise it is our fears that will gain ground, and our lives will be spent in their service. The good news is that even though this search for power over our fear is as old as humanity itself, so is the real solution: ours is the task of discovering that *our True Nature has nothing to fear.*

Start today, this very moment, to cut yourself loose from any fear that promises that freedom from its troubled presence will be found somewhere outside of you. Stop looking for an answer to what pains you; don't try to resolve the presence of a fear with the same mind that creates it. Instead, dare to act on your new understanding that nothing can threaten who you really are. Stand in the Light of Truth, and no shadows can touch you. Where is the need to protect yourself once you see that your True Nature is fearlessness itself?

See Through False Beliefs and Be Free

KEY LESSON

Don't wish for freedom; choose it. Start by challenging the
false notion that negativities are true powers. Deliberately
walk past any dark state whose painful presence—left
uncontested—makes you a prisoner of its domain.

First, a bit of good news: Reality is very different from our
often-troubled ideas about it. For instance, there are parts of us
that are secretly afraid that should we dive in and take a deeper
look at ourselves; we might stir up some things better left alone.
But Truth tells us differently. It says that if we don't bring all
that we are up into the Light of higher self-awareness, then we'll
lose the freedom born of discovering our fears are just "ghosts":
animated creations of a mind asleep to its own operation. The
following story illustrates this lesson in self-liberation:

It all happened in a quiet west Texas town called Turnaround
during the years of the Great Depression. This little town was
really quite ordinary in every sense of the word, except for one
thing: right in the heart of it stood an old haunted house.

Like most of the people who lived in the town, the four
young boys around whom our story centers did everything they
could to avoid passing by this run-down mansion. This was the
wise course to take! After all, the tales were legendary: anyone
foolhardy enough to venture too close to it would be dragged
inside by a ghoulish phantom! The boys had no wish for that
kind of an adventure, so they went considerably out of their

way each morning to walk down one of the other streets that would take them to school. No doubt it was inconvenient, but there was simply no other choice; no one in his right mind would pass by the menacing house!

Allow me to break into the story and draw the psychological parallel. We all have things inside of us that we fear: haunting thoughts and dark feelings we sense are down there, but that we'd rather not face for fear they may drag us into their domain. So, instead of questioning the right of these negative states to homestead in our souls, they dwell in the dark of us—living there virtually unchallenged.

What are these unseen apparitions whose presence we know, whose ache we conceal, but upon whose faces we won't look?

Isn't anger a kind of "demon"? Isn't despair at being alone a gloomy specter? And what about that phantom fear of growing old? Instead of looking at these internal chain-rattling entities to see whether or not they *really* have any power to hurt us, we keep them out of sight. Like the children in the town of Turn-around, we walk the other way whenever we distract ourselves from some unwanted condition or blame some outside cause for the way we feel.

All of this explains why the young boys in our story preferred to go the long way to school rather than challenge what they believed to be the perils of the haunted house. That is, all the boys except for one. His name was Justin.

And one fateful afternoon on the way home from school, just as they were all about to take their usual detour, Justin turned to his friends and asked, "How do we *know* that old house is actually haunted?"

With the exception of old stories and excitable hearsay, not one of his buddies had a real answer to his question other than to say, "Well, it just is."

But Justin was tired of going the long way around. He wanted to know, once and for all, the truth of the matter! It took some doing, but he convinced his schoolmates to approach the haunted house with him. Sure enough, it was just as predicted: as they drew closer, strange noises seemed literally to seep out of the walls. Shadows took on shapes, and a cold presence permeated the air itself. Here was proof that the house really was haunted!

The boys would have run, but the sound of Justin's voice—and the words he kept quietly speaking—held them steadfast.

"Nobody knows for sure," he kept telling himself over and over again. Armed and comforted with only his newfound uncertainty about the place, he ventured further up the weed-filled walk toward the front door that was already partly agape. Before he knew it, Justin had stepped inside. Meanwhile, his friends—who decided to wait in front of the porch steps—looked at each other in complete disbelief.

At first, the dim light, along with the tension of his drumming heart, caused Justin to jump at every strange noise. But as he dared to walk into each darkened corner to see what was causing the noises there, he soon began laughing out loud at his own fears. The only thing strange going on in that old house was the number of ways in which its old timbers would shudder from extreme old age, that's all. The wind passing through its weather-worn side boards made it howl. It really was pretty funny to think that nearly the whole town of Turnaround could have been so frightened by nothing!

A few minutes later, satisfied with his discoveries, Justin ran out into the light to tell his friends that there was nothing to be afraid of, but not one of them went in to see for himself. Each had his reason: it was late; tomorrow would be better; so on and so on. One boy even said he knew the house wasn't haunted all along.

Sure enough, the next day none of Justin's friends wanted to appear to be a coward, so they all walked with him past the old house on the way to school. But they never stopped looking over their shoulders, and they still jumped at each strange noise until the old house was out of sight. You see, they were secretly still afraid, because they had never found out the truth for themselves. Only Justin walked without fear because he knew the truth: *Nothing in that old house had any power to hurt him.*

There is only one way we can win this same freedom when it comes to the "house" of our self: we must agree to walk into and see through those mistaken beliefs of ours that are the secret source of our stress and fear. Following is a list of six false beliefs that betray all who look at their lives through these popular lies.

The purpose of this simple exercise is to help us see that the only thing that really "haunts" us is the degree to which we have agreed to live from certain social ideas that seem valuable but that leave us victims of the fear inherent in their pretext. The more conscious we can become of how these conditioned beliefs compromise our right to live without negative states, the more freedom we will win from them.

1. We are only as valuable, or worthless, as other people agree that we are.

2. We are responsible for the happiness or unhappiness that other people feel.
3. We can change what happened yesterday by reliving it today.
4. We must tolerate those people who have agreed to live with negative states.
5. We can only be as productive as we are willing to push ourselves through life.
6. We are as special, and important, as we feel stressed by our life.

For extra benefit, go back over each of these six points and answer the three simple questions that follow as you read each one. This extra effort on your part will prove invaluable, but you must do the exercise to be strengthened by it.

1. Is there any part of me that believes this statement is true?
2. What is the cost of any compromise I have made—to myself or others—to accommodate this belief of mine?
3. How many ways do I find myself justifying my actions to myself, or to others, for this belief?

One last word before we move on to our next section: during this exercise, embrace the Light by which you will see what is revealed to you. Choose to welcome your discoveries instead of resisting your reaction to them. Do this, and slowly, but surely, you'll realize nothing is more important in life than your growing relationship with the Truth that sets you free.

Adapted in part from
Who Put That Stone in My Shoe?

Three Revelations and Four Bright New Actions That Lead to the Fearless Life

KEY LESSON

Success born of anything less than hard work comes with the fear of losing what was never rightfully gained in the first place.

It's safe to say that most of us wrestle with some kind of frustration on a daily basis. This kind of dissatisfaction can be with ourselves, over what we can or can't get done, or with others, who may deny us our wish or otherwise disappoint our expectations. Accordingly, we can feel as though we are blocked, incapable, unable, not strong or wise enough to move ahead as we would like. The more we feel the unwanted presence of this limitation—accompanied as it always is by a host of painful dark thoughts and emotions—the more our attention is diverted to wrestle with *these troublesome states.* Without seeing it, our struggle is no longer with wanting to understand the cause of our situation, but is now with these negative states that *we don't want.* Feeling resentment over what we regret about ourselves makes sense only to the mind that believes soaking in a mud bath is the best way to get clean!

The real root of our daily frustration is not what it seems, which is why we have been unable, so far, to transcend its troubled presence within us. The secret source of our frustration in life is that we know intuitively, spiritually, that our True Self is created by the Limitless to live without limitation. But this doesn't mean what we imagine it to.... Actually, it means more than can be imagined. To understand this important idea about limitless, fearless living, we must get right down to fundamentals.

Most of us at least sense that whenever we fall into despair, lose our temper, or relive some past painful regret, we have lost possession of ourselves. To some extent we know that negative states limit our freedom because, in their dark presence, even our natural power of making proper choices is put to the test. And if our choices in such moments are (at least) in part produced by these self-limiting states, then how can what limits us help to free us of anything? It's obvious: it cannot. What are we to do?

We need a whole new and *true* understanding of what "living without limits" really means. It does *not* mean the power to manifest endless possessions or to access instant pleasures on demand. Even if one could achieve such ends, his or her life would still be fearfully empty for having to continually refill it with what must pass in time. What is limitless in life—*that which is without end within us*—is our God-given potential to transcend limitations. Let's take a simple example:

Those of us who have ever done any kind of work on strengthening our physical body know that at one point or another the body will tell us, "Enough! No more! I can't go any further!" We know by this pain or discomfort—especially when it comes to conditioning workouts—that our body is saying it has reached a certain limit beyond which it does not want to go. But, in the same moment, our past experience knows the body always "complains" when it doesn't want to go further than it's used to going. So, knowing that this pain is just part of what must be paid in order to grow stronger, we ignore the "warning" and push on to achieve the higher result we seek. Why do we make this choice? Because we understand, ahead of time, that this limit we have reached is only a temporary one; it is not the end of what is possible for us to do.

Now, can we see that this same reality must hold true regardless of whatever "body" in which we encounter such limitation—be it physical, psychological, or spiritual? When we reach the point where parts of us start to feel some kind of pain, some discomfort, it's not that there isn't more we could do; no, what limits us here is *what we are afraid to go through* in that moment.

What is it about this kind of fear that makes it so powerful? The answer may be hard to believe: Fear's power over us is nothing more than the way *it causes us to forget the truth of ourselves*, which is this: We are created to eternally transcend the limits of our present nature, to transform who and what we have been in the very moment it ceases to serve the good of us. But, because we have forgotten this, or—more accurately speaking—because we are asleep to its power in us, we are compelled to search for, find, and then believe in "powers" outside of ourselves that always betray us in our hour of need.

Actualizing our spiritual right to live without the frustration of fearful limitations is not a question of *achieving* something new; it begins with choosing to end a relationship with that which has never been true. So, it isn't a question of "What do I do?" but "What must I bring an end to?" Hence, the saying of Christ: "Whoever shall lose his life shall gain it."

Here for your consideration are three very common but false beliefs about what one must do or be in order to transcend the limitations in his or her life. Study them closely. See how their unquestioned, socially accepted convention serves both to frustrate and limit our natural right to be fearless. Also included with each example is a suggested new action whose purpose it is to help realize the limitless life of your True Self.

1. We must prepare—in advance—for everything that might happen to us.

   The world we live in "tells" us it is wise to worry, to stress ourselves over every eventuality, regardless of personal cost to our health, family, or friends. But recall here Christ's admonition, "Take no thought for the morrow." The truth is, the more we prepare to be fearless, the more afraid we become! Here's the new action to find the fearless life: *Meet every moment awake to what it wants to give to us: a life essentially limitless in its newness.* At the same time, detect and reject any fearful imagining about what might be lost should we step into the unknown moment before us.

2. Before we can make those real changes in our lives, the ones that will bring us the freedom we seek, we must first secure the approval of others for our actions.

   Most of us don't realize how dependent we are on the approval of others and how we weigh our life choices on scales that not only belong to others but that are broken as well. Here's the new liberating action: *Deliberately release any thought or feeling that would have us believe the freedom that we long for can be found by wearing the yoke of popular opinion.*

3. Before we can make—and then act upon—those new decisions that are needed to give new (and upward) direction to our lives, we must have our own approval.

   Now, add to these insights this last important fact: *All fear-producing false beliefs share one thing in common:*

Whenever we consider striking a long-overdue blow for our freedom—whether it's to walk away from an abusive relationship, start a new career, or maybe just spend more time by ourselves—*these fears only grant us their consent to move ahead* after *they've considered our proposed action in the light of what may become of us should we take it.* We can see this if we observe our thoughts closely in the appointed hour.

These discoveries prove one thing beyond the shadow of a doubt, even as they point to the need for a whole new action on our part: Since it's clear that who we have been up until now—our old nature— has no interest in helping us shake loose of its inherent limitations, we are left with only one conclusion that must be carried out through this bold new action: *We must lose all interest in protecting the interests of this fearful self.*

Reality itself is on our side in this struggle; Truth is our ally, and its Light empowers us to succeed, which means we can't lose. For instance, in any moment that some fear appears in our mind, and we remember that what we're seeing there is simply the dark spawn of negative imagination, then where is its power to push us around? That's right: the light of our realization in the moment needed is the same as dismissing that fear.

Here is one last encouraging, fear-busting fact and the bright action it helps to inspire. The source of our True Self is love-in-action. And since love transforms whatever it touches, any limitation can be transcended given our willingness to test this last truth: Our True Self is created neither to serve nor to believe in anything other than the living Light that is fearlessness itself. Prove this truth to yourself, and you will know its powers.

The Gentle Brush of Truth

KEY LESSON

Darkness thou art a subtle friend; if one knows thee full,
one knows thee naught.

If we could only remember—in the now—the fact that there
always come to us those telling moments when nothing that
mattered before matters as it once did; those times when the
things formerly valued are seen as being virtually without worth
to us, then . . .

Perhaps we might know our lives painted upon a broader
canvas, where our days would not be filled with their shallow
strokes of petty self-concerns, but with the gentle brush of what
is timeless and true.

And should we—for the sake of being present to ourselves in
the now—be able to see within ourselves this broad new scale
of Being, then we would also know that life itself has never
weighed in upon us so heavily as to hurt us; rather . . .

It was we—who in ignorance of reality—carelessly attributed
weight to events that were without substance, causing ourselves
to suffer nothing less than the fervent magnitude of our own
imagination.

SPECIAL KEY LESSONS IN REVIEW

1. Reliving some past pain with the idea that by doing so you won't have to go through that suffering again is like throwing money out the window so you won't spend it foolishly later on.

2. True fearlessness is knowing we are made for whatever happens to us whenever we are willing to let God remake us in that moment.

3. Fear is the bitter fruit that grows out of this unchallenged belief: Unless we struggle to satisfy our own desires, we shall never know fulfillment.

4. Fear and anger—as is true of all negative states—are "undercover agents." Their "soul" task, in any moment of conflict with life, is to rush in and cover up any possible impression that would otherwise reveal that we don't possess the "powers" to which we pretend.

5. Either we live in the freedom that we know is real—choosing to embody it in the moment, regardless of the cost—or we wave a flag called "liberty tomorrow" and suffer the indignity of serving what has already betrayed us.

Chapter 3

BREAK THROUGH THE ILLUSION OF LIMITATION

Illuminate and Liberate Yourself from Self-Limiting Thoughts and Feelings

KEY LESSON

Part 1   Whoever fails to try what his heart would have him do—because his mind tells him, "This you cannot do"—fails to hear the ever-present Voice of Reality forever shouting to all those who would dare: "No sincere effort ever goes without being rewarded."

Part 2   Never believe in any negative thought or feeling that would have you believe, "There's no way!" Always remember instead that real life is a secret and vital flux of possibilities rising up from the Ground of what seems improbable, much as a spring flower manages to bloom in a once-frozen field.

As the Light of higher self-knowledge dawns in us, we are able to see—in ever-greater clarity—the formerly unseen parts of ourselves that have held us captive. It's a paradox of the true spiritual path, but the more conscious we become of what limits us, the more limitless becomes our life. So, take as long as you need to understand the lesson that follows. It's intended to shed much-needed light on one of the more deceptive dark states that stands between us and the freedom for which we long.

The only purpose discouraged feelings serve is to keep your thoughts on *what you can't do*. And with your attention fixed in this fashion—on what seems impossible—there's no room for discovering what is possible—for *what you can do*.

Let's cover this important discovery one more time.

The only thing that feelings of discouragement do is *keep you busy doing nothing except feeling sorry for yourself,* which is the perfect guarantee that your sorry situation will remain hopelessly the same. Enough is enough! You don't have to put up with one more discouraging moment, let alone a life filled with its darkness. That's right. There is another choice you can learn to make besides falling into those familiar feelings of failure. Use this next higher idea to help you start thinking about those old discouragements in a new way.

Whenever we suffer over what we aren't able to do, have, win, or work through, our attention in these moments is riveted on our own thoughts, thoughts that are busy telling us we're somehow stuck. Maybe you can recognize some of these heavy-hearted inner voices. They say in one way or another . . .

- "I'll never get out of this mess."
- "I'm too stupid to learn these things."
- "I must have done something terrible to deserve this!"
- "There's no point in going any farther."
- "This is definitely hopeless."

Now, on the surface of things, these all-too-familiar whispers of defeat—these dark voices that reach our inner ears, speaking to us with our own voice—seem to be genuinely concerned with our unfortunate condition. But a deeper look into this covert operation reveals these troubled thoughts are up to something totally different. There is an unseen "conspiracy of limitation" taking place within our own consciousness! Follow the next four ideas all the way to their stunning conclusion. They show us that self-illumination and self-liberation are one and the same power.

1. The more these gloomy voices talk to us, the more discouraged we feel.
2. The more discouraged we feel, the more certain we are that we have no other choice but to feel that way.
3. The more convinced we are that we have no choice, *the less choice we have.*
4. The act of identifying with this dark inner dialogue actually produces the dead end we fear!

We end up being able to go no farther with our wish for broader personal horizons because, unbeknownst to ourselves, we now believe that there's no way to get past where *we now perceive ourselves to be limited* or tied down. The key idea in this part of our investigation lies within the word *perceive,* because—for the purposes of this exercise—the word *perceive* rhymes with *deceive.* And that's precisely what this faulty perception is: a self-deception. Here's proof.

There are no dead ends in real life. Of course you must prove this bright fact to yourself, and here's a good place to start: in any given moment, there is always something higher you can do with your life than sit there and suffer over what you think you can't have, or do, or be. Why wallow when a small amount of interior work will act to change your reality?

Here's one example of a new and higher inner action to take when faced with the presence of any discouraging inner state: *See that the size of the discouragement you feel is directly proportional to the size of your insistence that life conform to your demands.* Then, having verified this truth for yourself, dare to quietly drop that self-defeating demand.

The first time you bring such a light to bear on any discouraged thought or feeling, it will fade from view—much as shadows do when the sun reaches its midday zenith. Their departure leaves you with fresh new energies that not only grant you "new eyes" through which to see how you can proceed with your wish, but that also grant you the strength to begin the next leg of your quest.

For instance, maybe you've felt discouraged because you wanted to learn something new—a higher skill or a difficult lesson—but felt sure that certain limitations of yours placed this possibility beyond your abilities. And so you resigned yourself to feeling discouraged. While this kind of self-defeating behavior is commonly accepted as natural, it's totally unnecessary. You can do something much higher!

Instead of falling into those familiar feelings of futility over yourself, work to deliberately drop those discourage-filled thoughts that are telling you the limit of your present view is the limit of your possibilities. Who you *have been* matters only to those dark states that want you to remain that way so that they can continue to rule the day. Refuse to dwell in discouragement over who your own thoughts are telling you you'll never be. Just get started working on who, and what, you are right now!

In other words, *do what's in your power and refuse to be discouraged about anything else.* And keep repeating this new conscious action one step at a time, over and over again. *It is* in your power to learn whatever it takes—one lesson at a time—and make it all the way to your designated goal.

Here's one last special thought to help summarize this important life lesson in liberating ourselves from the limitations of discouragement:

Any conversation you permit yourself to have with dark and discouraging thoughts guarantees you'll wind up with a dozen good reasons for why you feel so dark and discouraged. **When it comes to any negative thought, the first word you have with it is the same as giving it the last word with *you*.**

Practice these higher lessons in self-liberation until you're free of all feelings of futility. You'll soon see how this new action gives you the last laugh on discouragement.

Go Beyond Thinking and Stop Sinking

KEY LESSON

Part 1 Calling on anxious thoughts to check the rising tide of some fearful feeling is like trying to stop a landslide by throwing rocks at it!

Part 2 Using thought as a tool to resolve the troubles that thought stirs up in the mind is like trying to use your fingers to seize, sort, and settle dust particles that are dancing in a sunbeam across your living room floor.

Too frequently we feel as though our lives are under the power of things outside of us and beyond our ability to deal with: we are prisoners in one way or another of an unfair social system, impossible work conditions, an unforgiving past, or a failed relationship. Even trying to assemble a build-it-yourself book-shelf that doesn't know it "goes together with ease" can lock us away in the house of pain.

Whatever the antagonist, our response is pretty standard: we resist, struggling to get out from under what we see as standing over us. However, the fact of the matter is things are not as they seem. *No event of itself has power;* it is we who unconsciously color the moments of our lives with the unhappy quality of character that we then turn around and lament for being there. Let's examine this important idea, so that we can begin liberating ourselves from what amounts to an unseen act of self-limitation.

Our experience of any passing event—for the pain or pleasure of it—is *the product of how we see it.* This principle is a timeless spiritual truth: the inner determines the outer, which simply means that our experience of life is one and the same with how we perceive it. So, as astonishing as it may seem at first, it's true: The *only* power any unwanted moment holds over us is the power we give to it. Think what this means, beginning with this vital idea that points directly to the possibility of never again having to feel like a victim.

Negative states are not mandatory; believe it or not, *they are voluntary!* Proving this to ourselves is the first step in walking out of the psychological prison created by our current misperception of reality, so let's get started.

Emotional pain is not an intrinsic part of any event, any more than gathering darkening clouds means an inescapable depression is coming.

The light of this insight changes everything, starting with the age-old question, "How do we free ourselves from 'powers' that seem greater than ourselves?" Now we know where to look for the answer: emancipation begins with our willingness to explore and expose the invisible workings of the false self that keeps us its captive. The following example will make everything crystal clear.

Imagine for a moment you're driving home from work, and you've just come from having a pretty rough day at the office. As you drive along, your eyes see the road before you, but your mind is in the past. It's very busy running and then rerunning a few of the day's unpleasant events, much like an unattended slideshow cycling through the same few images over and over again. You relive that painful stab of some thoughtless remark someone cruelly blurted out, or the embarrassment of that stupid comment you made without thinking.

All we need to see to be able to walk out of this darkened theatre of unhappy thoughts is right before our eyes: the more we think, *the more we sink!* Instead of achieving the freedom we imagine will result from this struggle, we find ourselves further entangled in the dark web of our own imagination!

In moments such as these, our lives and our choices are not our own; they are literally the property of a mind that is asleep to its own operations. Its unique "blindness" is that *it's busy showing itself the very images that it doesn't want to look at!* This means the more desperately the mind struggles to escape the conflict it feels, the less it's able to realize that *its real struggle is with itself*—and not with the world that it blames for its conflicted condition.

As we are now beginning to see, breaking free of this interior web of thought can't happen by pulling on the individual strands of thought that hold us there. In the end, it is *awareness* of our actual dilemma that releases us from it. By its light we are empowered to see the truth about our "thought self" and the false sense of life it weaves for itself by thinking about itself: *its world is not the same as ours.*

Like the swan that mistook itself to be an ugly duckling until it caught a glimpse of its own graceful reflection in still waters, we can open our interior eyes and see that the world of thought is not the home of our True Self. This practice is called self-observation. It is "the alpha and the omega" of a life without limits, because through it we realize that who we really are cannot be confined by anything, let alone a cage of thought.

Learning to observe our self begins with one simple but deliberate act of attention on our part. As many times a day as we can remember to do it, we want to first come awake to whatever activity is running through our own mind, and then simply, quietly, *take a single step back from our own thoughts.* We *watch* our own thinking—its movement and character—instead of allowing ourselves to be drawn onto its stage and into its drama.

Our foremost wish is to witness what our false self is busy spinning out of thought so that we don't fall into its web; instead of reacting to these thoughts and feelings as they pass through us, pulling us into their world as they do, we release them *as they are being formed.* In other words, we are neither for, nor against, any thought with any other thought. And should we find ourselves sinking into the web of some needless negative thinking, we need only step back and watch *that* event. Although thought is sticky stuff, please know—in spite of appearances—release is immediate! So, we must stick with our new intention to "see" our way free until we know the truth of it in the moment.

If we agree to start over and over again with this interior practice, here is the glad discovery we can't help but make: Higher self-awareness, through self-observation, puts us in direct contact with a new and superior intelligence that already lives within us; and through its steady silent wisdom we realize a new kind of strength that is always there when we need it.

This living Light sees the mindless self-serving antics of our false self from a thousand miles away—which is the same as lifting us above its web of limitations. By this Light we see for ourselves *what is real and what is not,* which is the same as saying negative states no longer have the power to hold us down because we can no longer be deceived into mistaking their world for that of our own.

Letting Go of What Limits Our Relationships

KEY LESSON

Most people pounce on other people as they do—when they do—not because they want to cause pain, but because they're afraid of being hurt. To see this truth is to realize that the real enemy of a relationship is fear itself; for this dark state that dwells in the unenlightened heart knows that the best way to protect itself is by being first to find fault with another.

No relationship in life can be any more successful than what we are willing to learn about ourselves through it. The moment we turn our back on what others give us to see about ourselves, we not only walk away from what we need to see, *but also from the better person we could be* . . . were we only willing to learn the lesson at hand.

The success of our relationships with others—and that must include all we're intended to realize about ourselves through them—depends on a two-part key that unlocks our potential to love: First, we are asked to do the interior work of becoming aware of ourselves in a whole new way. Second, we must learn to welcome what this new light reveals to us about ourselves. One without the other is useless.

Sadly enough, due to the mass marketing of spiritual ideas and the glut of iconic imagery that goes with that, many people these days believe they are already self-aware and "living in the Light." So, the first step for those of us wishing to escape the painful limitations of any harmful relationship with another— or with our own present nature—begins with admitting the following to ourselves: Yes, we have the awareness we need to "get through" life and to resolve many of its issues, but this power to rationalize the world we walk through is only part of the whole story: our continuing conflict with others—as well as within our own heart and mind—clearly reveals that this level of awareness is not enough.

The late great mystic Vernon Howard, a spiritual giant, had a favorite saying when it came to seeing the truth about our present level of development. He would often tell his students, "The medicine is bitter, but it heals!" It's true; and so is the fact that nearly all of humanity is asleep to itself; six and a half-billion "sleepwalkers" who—even as they move through life—are all but oblivious to the reality of the invisible worlds within them that are shaping their lives.

It is to help us discover this unseen state of our Self that authentic spiritual "exercises" came to exist and have been passed along down through the ages. Their true purpose was never to empower human beings with what the sleeping mind dreamed would rescue it, but to awaken the "sleeper" within—the True Self—*to its unnatural state of imprisonment. True illumination is liberation from the illusion of passing time and the world of thought that creates it.*

So, the purpose of any true interior practice is not to help us "do" or achieve something in the world that will make our future a brighter one, but to help us *see something now about our present level of being.* But our wish and work to be aware of ourselves isn't just to see ourselves through this Light of higher awareness, but also to *allow its celestial presence to act upon us.*

We cannot change ourselves; nothing in the created universe can make itself greater than it already is. This means our responsibility is not to try and enhance ourselves through our various relationships in life, but rather to discover and realize ourselves through them. Think of the vast difference between these two pursuits. One brings endless ways in which we feel we must make painful compromises with others in order to protect what we have "gained" through them. The other way leads us to the gradual realization of an interior greatness that can neither be enslaved nor corrupted. Only our awakening can end the aching inherent in the many ways we have become falsely dependent upon others. Those who depend on others to provide them with their sense of worth are codependent;

each *must* have the other to keep the illusion alive, even though by feeding this relationship they effectively separate themselves from the possibility of ever knowing their true value.

Here's the point: Anyone we enable, *we disable* ... including ourselves. And there's only one reason any two people consent to compromise themselves in this way: neither has yet discovered the truth of who they really are. Now let me restate a spiritual law:

We can never enable someone else without having first disabled our own higher nature that knows better than to bargain for friendship, love—or just to feel "needed" in some way. Resentment and regret are the bitter fruit of all codependent relationships, because the ground out of which they grow is self-compromise disguised as caring for one another. We cannot authentically care for another until we carry within us the lighted lamp of higher self-understanding.

A big part of our inner work in all of our relationships involves remembering this key idea: Whenever we are not present and properly attentive to ourselves, we may be sure the false self is busy attending to something we'll be paying for in the days ahead. Disconcerting, yes; but there's no denying it: there are unconscious parts of us that feel good about getting us to do wrong! No form of codependent behavior thrives without an unseen character at work within us, providing it with the conditions it needs to flourish.

Any time we enable another—cause them to wrongly depend upon us—or, conversely, depend upon someone else to "comfort" us for what we give them in exchange, we have limited the lives of all involved. Of course we're not conscious of what we are doing, or we wouldn't involve ourselves with others in this way. Which brings us to the examples that follow.

Welcome these next insights, which are taken from my book, *Beyond Dependency*. Let your intuition instruct you as to how to apply the lessons they impart. Use their light to help you see some of the invisible ways in which we not only enable but spiritually disable friends, family, loved ones, and ourselves.

Making "Peace" with People Who Would Punish Us

There are parts of us that would rather be punished by unkind people than have to spend one minute being alone, because the only way these same parts in us can exist is if they have someone to resent or somehow fear. In this case we remain in these ruinous relationships because the fear or emptiness we feel in even considering leaving them seems to be too much to bear on our own.

Here's the key to escaping this captivity: This familiar fear—of being alone in life—feels real, no doubt; but *it belongs to an imagined self.* We must now act on what we know is the truth of our condition, instead of remaining its captive. Translation: Walk away from anyone who "helps" you to feel that it's necessary for you to hurt; leave anyone who causes you pain for "your own good." Here's the rule to remember: Never accept as natural or necessary any relationship outwardly—or inwardly—with a person or psychological state that punishes you. Say "No" and just go! A whole new and independent life awaits you.

Blaming Others

Whenever we allow angry parts of us to cast blame on others for the conditions we find ourselves in, we enable the false self to keep dreaming that if it weren't for others doing us wrong we would never feel so angry, defeated, or depressed.

The truth is there are unconscious parts of us that readily find fault with others in a misguided effort to remain infallible in our own eyes. Each time we blame someone else, we agree to remain asleep in this misery-making mistaken identity. Saying "No" to this nature is saying good-bye to a host of imagined enemies this false self needs to remain itself, as well as to a war that can never be won.

What should be clear now is that we have to do a special kind of inner work if we wish to catch and cancel self-harming codependent behavior. It's not enough to just talk about achieving a good, contented life. Anyone can talk about that, and most do. Few will really do the interior work it takes to be free, which is why we must be different.

We must learn to put the Light of Truth before all things. No such effort ever goes unrewarded. Little by little the living Light reveals within us a new and higher order of strength that has no problem saying "No" to those unconscious parts of us that care for nothing and no one, not even themselves! This new "No" then becomes a "Yes" to self-wholeness—the secret source of all healthy, happy, and unlimited relationships.

Adapted from *Beyond Dependency*

Invite the Light That
Shatters Self-Limitation

KEY LESSON

We are not created to spend our lives in fearful preparation over what may come—but rather to use whatever comes our way, each moment, to help us perfect our understanding that God is good.

In those moments when we meet a challenge that stands in our way, we are not meeting some immovable, transient object. In reality, we are meeting nothing more than our own present understanding of that event. *Wherever we are—whatever we encounter—we meet there our own understanding.*

This is such an important insight for us to ponder: the dimension—the breadth and depth of any event transpiring before us—is a reflection of the level of self that perceives it. In other words, life cannot be any deeper, wiser, shallow, or selfish than permitted by what we are capable of understanding about it.

There is such beauty and freedom in this realization about the nature of our reality: we look at life through the mirror of our consciousness, and what we see there—whether all bound up or boundless—is determined by our present level of self-understanding. In other words, whenever our present nature meets some barrier, a limit of any kind, all it's really run up against is itself. *The self that sees limitation . . . is the limitation it sees;* this is why it can't see past that point! It *is* the "end" it sees; they are one thing.

On the other hand, true spiritual success is one and the same as our realization that, in real life, nothing ends without the birth of something else taking place in that same moment.

Our True Self is the creative Ground of a ceaseless genesis; our great task in life—through our awareness of the whole of it—is to be a kind of midwife to this eternal miracle of birth. And what is continually being born in us and into this world of ours—whether for its bitterness or brightness—depends on how we meet these changes that drive creation forward. Let's see how these grand ideas reveal themselves in our daily affairs.

As life pours itself out in the stream of passing time, and we run into challenges seemingly greater than our ability to answer, each of these encounters "asks" this question of us:

"Are you willing to change (who you have been) in order to realize a higher possibility of yourself?"

And though moments like these trouble us because of their uncertainty, here's why we should be very grateful for their continuing appearance in our lives: *this unwanted experience of realizing our limitations is the only way life can ask us if we wish to go beyond them.* So this unknown moment of not understanding (what is to be) is actually the beautiful seed of a new order of our being, providing we're willing to see it as such.

Unfortunately, most of us automatically resist the unknown. Whenever we can't understand the nature of some unwanted situation, we fall, by default, into the hands of a nature whose answer to this ache is always the same: get negative and then try to protect ourselves from anything that can't be otherwise controlled. The rest takes place in us on automatic pilot: in the wink of an eye, we begin to see the "way out" of our situation: blame him, fix that, fight or flee. But here's what we don't see:

in that moment, our guiding light is a dark reaction dedicated, in one way or another, to avoiding what that moment came to give us. This false nature takes what was a celestially planned event—for the purpose of our further spiritual perfection—and turns it into a dead end.

We have all heard about people receiving messages, instructions from God. What you probably don't realize is that "communications of a celestial kind" are raining down on us every waking moment. In fact, each impression we receive—wanted or not—is just that: the Divine Life speaking to us, asking, "Would you like entrance into a larger world, one without fear and hatred? Do you wish to be more patient, loving, and kind? Are you interested in developing a relationship with a living Light that never goes out, and whose peace passes all understanding?" But before we can hope to affirm our answer, we must first see how these questions are being put before us.

Life repeatedly brings us moments that introduce us to some unseen limitation in our present level of self. For example, when conditions get too stressful, we can keep neither our patience nor our temper under control. Too often, though we know better, cruel words spring from our mouth as our way of answering cutting remarks from someone else. Perhaps we see how the fear of being betrayed (again) colors all our relationships, limiting our ability to give ourselves freely to those we would love.

The point should be clear: Time and time again, interior trials such as these return to help us see one thing: we can't get past them as long as we remain who and what we have been—*because who and what we have been is what we are meeting in these same moments!* Another way of stating this same insight is startling: Resisting what life shows us—not wanting those moments wherein we're invited to see the truth about our present level of self—ensures they will return again! This is the interior meaning of reincarnation: the recreation of self through resistance to the negative effects of its own manifestations. It doesn't have to be this way. We are meant to rise above creation, not repeat our life through it in ever-descending cycles.

There's only one way for us to transcend the limitations of our present nature. We must see—as has been the purpose of this whole lesson—this one great fact: *These limitations don't belong to us* any more than the clumsy body of the caterpillar belongs to the butterfly liberated from its husk. Then, we must act on this new understanding by daring to let go of any part of us that wants us to embrace its limited view of life as our own.

True freedom is not an achievement; it is our awakened relationship and participation with the genesis of real life. We cannot create a life without limits by trying to overcome what we think stands in our way. Real limitless living is the fruit of this higher understanding: *what is in our way is part of the Way.* To know this is to know that all of creation has been made for you, just as surely as you have been made for everything that happens to you within it.

The Secret of Having Everything
You Want

KEY LESSON

If we work each moment to practice kindness, patience, and persistence—doing so in grateful remembrance that each breath we take is a gift—here's what we'll find: the power of being present in this way ensures that each of our "tomorrows" dawns with more Light than was seen this day.

Everyone wonders whether or not there is one Great Secret for truly successful living. There is. And it is not a secret. It has been quietly, steadily telling itself right in front of us all along. We just couldn't hear it over the clatter and chatter of our own demands. Listen quietly for a moment. Everything can change right now. Learning to hear this Supreme Secret is no more difficult than choosing whether to swim against a current or to let it carry you safely to the shore. Let it speak its wisdom to that secret part of you that cannot only hear what it is saying but that is, in reality, its very voice. Listen to it now. It is saying, "Want what life wants." Think about it. Locked within these four simple words is the secret of an uncompromising power for effortless living; a new kind of power that never fails to place you on the winning side of any situation. Why? Because when you want what *Life wants,* your wish is for Life itself.

"What if I don't like what Life brings to me?"

"Try to see that it is not what Life has brought to you that you don't like. It is your reactions that turn the gift of Life into the resentment of it."

"I don't want to sound ungrateful, but speaking plainly, I'm tired of being unhappy. What difference does it make why I feel this way?"

"Because these unhappy feelings are born out of Life failing to conform to your ideas of what you need to be happy. This shows you, if you will see it, that Life itself isn't denying you happiness. It is your ideas about Life that have failed you. Give up these wrong ideas instead of giving up on Life. Be increasingly willing to see that they are nothing but a constant source of conflict. Your false nature will tell you that you must have these self-protecting ideas; that you can't live without them or you will lose something valuable. What you must do, in spite of any such protest to the contrary, is to see that you can't live with them. All you will lose is your unhappiness."

Here are two lists that not only will make these life-healing ideas more personal for you, but that will help you to make a higher choice when it comes to what you really want from life. It would be valuable to study and then compare the lists to each other. You may wish to add to either list some of your own insights, which I highly encourage you to do.

Let's look at what happens *when you want what you want:*

1. You are often nervous and anxious because life may not cooperate with your plans.
2. You are willing to sacrifice whatever it takes to get what you want, and this may include your integrity.
3. You are usually scheming in some way to win your next victory.

4. You are either in a battle or recovering from one.
5. You are unable to rest quietly when you need to.
6. You are easily angered when someone or something gets in your way.
7. You are forever driven to want something else.
8. You are against anyone else who also wants what you want.
9. You are certain that what you have is who you are.
10. You are always trying to convince yourself that you got what you want.

Now carefully consider what happens *when you want what life wants:*

1. You are never disappointed with what happens.
2. You are always in the right place at the right time.
3. You are quietly confident no matter what the circumstances.
4. You are out of the reach of anger and anxiety.
5. You are awake and sensitive to your surroundings.
6. You are free of ever feeling as though you've missed out.
7. You are never thrown for a loss.
8. You are in total command of events.
9. You are mentally quiet.
10. You are eternally grateful.

"Is there a simple guideline to follow when it comes to distinguishing between what Life wants and what I want? How can I easily tell which is which?"

"Always remember the following. If any want is the source of anxiety or sorrow, that want is yours and not

Life's. If the want has pain, it is in vain. To let real life flood in, pull yourself out of the flood of self-wants that promise a future pleasure but only deliver a present pain."

"How do I pull myself out of the flood of my own wants?"
"See that you are being washed away by them and you will grow tired of being bounced along. Here is a key. Never accept the presence of any mental or emotional suffering as necessary, no matter how much importance these impostors lend to a particularly pressing want. By refusing their dark presence, you make space for the real Present. This is where the Life you want and that wants you is waiting."

Let Life bring you itself. Welcome it. At each instant, it is new, full—untouched and undiminished by any moment before it. To enter into this full relationship with Life is to give yourself to your Self. Fulfilling the true purpose of Life is fulfilling yourself. They are one and the same. *Want what life wants.*

Adapted in part from *The Secret of Letting Go*

SPECIAL KEY LESSONS IN REVIEW

1. The true source of abundance is the silent mind, for in its fertile quietude rests all potential, all power, and all promise.

2. The past is as powerless to darken the present moment as is a shadow to reach up and drag down the form that casts it.

3. No one is free who thinks that he is; he is free alone who no longer has any need to think about himself at all.

4. Work to connect yourself to the "allness" of life, instead of identifying with the smallness of it, and you'll awaken to a greatness already living within you that is no more bothered by the little things in life than a mountain is made miserable by the rain that falls upon it.

5. Your True Self cannot be made a captive of any dark condition any more than a sunbeam can be caught in a bottle.

Chapter 4

TAKE CONSCIOUS
COMMAND OF YOURSELF

The Secret Path to the Summit
of Your Self

KEY LESSON

Spiritual wisdom is our greatest wealth, and as we realize
the truth of this—so that true self-knowledge becomes our
single greatest wish in life—each moment of every one of
our relationships serves as the secret path to the summit
of ourselves.

Not too many years ago, there was a party game that involved
one person telling another what animal the other person most
resembled, either by appearance or by character. As you might
imagine, some players were pleased to be seen as the fierce lioness
or great bear. On the other hand, those who qualified as mouse,
snake, or walrus types didn't much appreciate how others perceived them!

Now, if we were to take the whole human race and try to
see its nature as being one creature, what kind of animal comes
to mind for you? For me, the answer is evident: humankind
most resembles an ostrich. When a disturbance comes along,
this creature sticks its head in the sand so as not to see what's
taking place. This is not unlike closing our eyes in the hope
that an approaching tiger won't see us! The rationale behind
this study in stupidity is the terribly mistaken idea that what we
don't know—what we don't see—about ourselves won't hurt us.
And, as with any comforting superstition, the ignorance behind
it always finds ways to justify the suffering that attends living
from a false belief. In this instance, when we find ourselves in
a dark state over a situation we'd rather not deal with, our pain

"proves" to us that we are not at fault, because we would never do that to ourselves!

Let's summarize this unhappy condition, as well as glimpse what's needed to take command of it: *Instead of being self-discovering—as we are created to be—we are self-deceiving.* Our present level of consciousness lives in a shaky alliance with a host of dark states that betray us by making it seem as though we can delay dealing with what we fear about ourselves. Why would any of us choose to lose in this way when we are the creation of a fearless Light, endowed with the right to command all that happens within us?

The answer is as simple as it can be hard to see: through countless generations of mounting false social, cultural, and corrupted religious traditions, we've been conditioned to believe in a lie that looks something like this: *Whatever character faults we fear dwell within us must not only be hidden from the world around us, but kept from ourselves as well.*

This unconscious conclusion is not only a tragedy, but unchecked, it is a prescription for psychic pain that will never end. Here is the real medicine:

We are created to be self-correcting beings through our awareness of whatever we see within us that is needful of being corrected.

This doesn't mean we judge ourselves; condemning ourselves only keeps us a captive of the false self that sits in judgment of everything. Instead, we simply agree to let the Light of higher perception do its work of perfecting us in ways we can't imagine. In no time at all we realize that being enlightened is always better than living frightened! Better still, when nothing is left within us that can deceive us into resisting its dark presence, causing us to act against ourselves, we rule ourselves. In short, *we are granted true command over our lives in direct proportion to our willingness to be conscious of it as it unfolds within us.* This idea—that a new and higher awareness of ourselves holds the power we need to change our lives—is as exciting as it is challenging to understand. After all, as so many ask upon hearing these new ideas, "Where does one begin?"

Here's a great place to start: ask yourself whether those thoughts and feelings that want you to feel *any* form of despair are for or against your happiness. Such a question, asked sincerely, is a form of Light; for just by asking to see the truth of these things you will start to see—without any further effort — this astonishing fact: these punishing states of yourself may be familiar, but *they are not your friends!*

Strange as it may sound at first, there are many parts of us that would prefer we never discover the following: The universe is created for the purpose of helping us to realize our True Self. Our role in this celestial process of creation perfecting itself is twofold: first we need to *awaken* to the existence of this Divine plan; then we are asked to *consent* to its most intimate work within us. Fortunately, this is a natural progression of interior events, for the discovery of our inheritance compels us to receive it; and one of the gifts born in our growing awareness of this secret holiness to life is greater self-command. After all, once we see that nothing can happen to us that isn't already a part of this perfection in motion, what is there to fear?

The birth of this new strength is, in part, what it means to walk through life with "Truth by our side." For now we are starting to live from a wisdom that "passes all understanding." Our new vision shows us, even in the midst of what used to make us miserable, that *everything we encounter is for the good of us.* And the light of this new and higher self-understanding shines in all places, including those parts of us we would rather never run into: hatefulness, jealousy, regret, despair, rage—whatever that shadow may be that makes us want to look away from it.

Here is where the Light of higher self-knowledge steps in to show us how we are being deceived. And, as we will see by this same Light, its revelation is the same as our release.

As a rule, the first thing we experience—whenever we see something negative in us—is an involuntary negative reaction: we immediately condemn ourselves. But *Light never condemns;* its nature is to reveal, transform, and release. Which means this mechanical mental activity going on in us—along with its aching—must be going on for some purpose other than our perfection or protection. What's it trying to cover up?

Whenever we identify with a negative reaction about something negative we have seen within us, where is our attention? The answer is that it's on the pain we feel over having seen our imperfection. Which means we are no longer aware of what has caused this suffering, because we are now identified with the suffering itself. And with our awareness now focused on this disturbance—looking at what we wish we were not—the real culprit behind our conflict slips away, back into the unconsciousness from which it came. That dark character "knows" the only chance it has to remain at large within us is if it can trick us into covering it up with some other form of darkness like fear, shame, or self-loathing. In this bit of twisted logic, we are made to feel that condemning ourselves for what we see is the first step toward a cure for that unwanted condition. This is a lie that serves only the continuity of that dark character. *What is condemned is concealed; what is concealed never heals.* Real interior healing can take place only in the moment we become conscious of the need for it, and only the Light that reveals this need has the power to change what it has revealed.

Whenever we catch a glimpse of something dark dwelling within us, we do so by the grace of a living Light. Its wish is to give us what we cannot give to ourselves: true spiritual freedom and its peaceable command over all our interior states. It offers us this greatest of gifts by inviting us to bring whatever we see about ourselves *into the light of its Life.* As we do this, our former dread of darkness fades away, because the fear that bred it no longer holds power over us. We see—beyond the shadow of any doubt—that it is never negative to see the negative, since it is always the perfectly positive that empowers us with this new kind of seeing.

Stop This Secret Self-Sabotage

KEY LESSON

The true individual is no more concerned over what others may think of him or her than is the sun troubled by people complaining that it's too hot!

We're often led to act against ourselves by an undetected weakness that goes before us—trying to pass itself off to others—as a strength. In effect, we pretend to be something we're not—

a commonly accepted behavior these days. But any time we feign anything, we do so out of fear that without that "persona" to protect us—to make that impression we want—we won't get what we want. This whole way of thinking is secret self-sabotage. It sinks us in our personal and business relationships as surely as a torpedo wrecks the ship it strikes. Learning how to stop this self-sinking is the focus of this section. As always, the best way to begin any journey of self-discovery is to gather the Light we'll need to succeed. Your consideration of the two special insights that follow will start you down the path to a whole new kind of self-command.

1. Any person you feel the need to control or dominate—so that he or she will treat you as you "think" you should be treated—will always be in charge of you ... and treat you accordingly. Why? Because *anyone from whom you want something, psychologically speaking, is always in secret command of you.*

2. Any action you take to appear strong before another person is actually read by that person as a weakness. If you doubt this finding, review the past interactions and results of your own relationships. The general rule of thumb is that *the more you demand or crave the respect of others, the less likely you are to receive it.* If you've ever tried to raise children, you know this is true. So it makes no sense to try and change the way others treat you by learning calculated behaviors or attitude techniques in order to appear in charge. The only thing these clever cover-ups really produce is yet another source of secret inner conflict, which, in turn, only fuels further

self-sabotage. Besides, what you're really looking for in your relationships isn't command over others—but over yourself. So what's the answer?

Stop trying to be strong. Instead, *catch yourself when you are about to act from weakness.*

Don't be too surprised by this unusual instruction. A brief examination reveals its wisdom. Following are ten examples of how you may be secretly sabotaging yourself while wrongly assuming you're strengthening your position with others.

1. Fawning before people to win their favor
2. Expressing contrived concern for someone's well-being
3. Making small talk to cover up nervousness
4. Hanging on to someone's every word
5. Looking for someone's approval
6. Asking if someone is angry with you
7. Fishing for a kind word
8. Trying to impress someone
9. Gossiping
10. Explaining yourself to others

Let's examine this last act of secret self-sabotage: the compulsive need to explain ourselves to others, even when no one has asked us to do so!

The next time you feel as though you need to explain yourself to someone (other than to your employer, as it may concern his or her business affairs), give yourself a quick and simple internal test. This test will help you check for and cancel any undetected weakness that's about to make you sabotage yourself. Here's how to get started: run an interior pressure check.

Right at the outset of the moment in question, usually just bumping into someone, come as wide awake to yourself as is possible for you to be. Allow the inner Light of this heightened awareness to scan the various shaky states passing through you, and then, safe within its calmness, silently ask yourself this question: Is that personal question you're about to answer—or that answer you're about to give, without having been asked for it—something you really want to do? Or are you about to explain yourself because you're afraid of some as yet undisclosed consequence if you don't?

This self-administered test for inner pressure is how you tell if your forthcoming explanation is truly voluntary, or if you're on the verge of being compelled unconsciously to compromise your own integrity.

Your awareness of any pressure building within you is the proof that it's some form of fear—and not you—that wants to do the explaining, fawning, impressing, blabbing, or whatever that self-sabotaging inner pressure is pushing you to commit. Each time you feel this pressurized urge to give yourself away, silently but solidly refuse to release this pressure by giving into its demands. It may help you to succeed sooner if you know that fear has no voice unless it tricks you into giving it one. Choosing inner seeing over the wish to be seen by others in a complimentary light stops the cycle of self-sabotage.

Adapted in part from Design Your Destiny

Take This One Step and Stay Out of Trouble

KEY LESSON

Count the number of ways in which we have acted to protect a fear—as in fawning before others for fear of falling out of their good graces —and we also know the exact number of times we have been the fool of fear.

There was once a young prince who, having reached the age of majority, left home to live on a grand estate given to him by his father. He was told that if he ever needed help he was to put a light in the uppermost tower window, and his father would send a special horse and carriage to carry him to safety.

However, his father also warned him that an evil wizard, an enemy of the kingdom, lived not too far from his new home. The prince was told to be wary when setting his signal, for this wizard would also see this light and might himself send his own horse and carriage to carry the prince off to who knows what kind of danger. Of course, this frightened the young ruler-to-be. After all, how would he be able to tell the difference? His father assured him there was a foolproof measure. Each time, before entering the rescue carriage, he was to closely examine the horse pulling it. A light-colored horse would always take him to safety, but a dark horse would always take him to danger.

As one might imagine, many of the ordeals that come with the ruling life befell the prince, each one causing him to put a light in the window. And for many months, because he was in such a rush to escape his castle when he felt in danger, he failed to heed his father's warning; time and time again he neglected to examine the horse that came to get him. As a result he often found himself on one painful wild ride after another where, too late, he realized his inattentiveness was causing him as much distress as the condition he was trying to escape. Eventually, he found the presence of mind—*before* he would get into the carriage that had come for him—to see if the horse pulling it had been sent by the evil wizard or by his father. His growing ability to recognize and refuse the "dark horse" kept him safe.

This little truth tale is deceptively simple, but before you discount its power to help you, please consider that the only responses to life's challenges that any of us "ride" are those we think can carry us to safety. Leaping onto the back of these reactions, according to our old habits, is like entering a runaway carriage being pulled along by runaway thoughts and pounding feelings. Fortunately, like the prince, we can learn to shed the light of reality upon these responses before we look to them to carry us to a safe place. Let's look more closely at this possibility for higher self-protection.

It is not necessary to continue being defeated by our own mechanical responses. We can learn to recognize a dark-horse reaction before we are carried away by it. We already know what many of these runaway reactions are, so the battle is half-won. Fear is dark. Anger is dark. So are anxiety, dread, self-pity, and feeling the whole weight of the world upon our shoulders. Add to this list the dark horses of hatred, revenge, insistence on being right, impatience, and depression—and you have most of those negative states that, if not outright trampling us under their heartless hooves, are certainly sources of unconscious torment.

So you see, knowing the difference between a horse sent by the evil wizard and a horse sent by the good king is not that complicated. It is as simple as recognizing that the wrong horse hurts because its real purpose is to take you on a punishing, pounding ride. You can be sure you've taken the wrong horse and carriage whenever your inner state has you feeling:

- Like you've lost control
- Frightened by what you see
- Angry with yourself or another person
- Confused or anxious about where you're headed
- Pained in your present position
- Hatred or resentment for someone else
- Sorry you were ever born
- Envious of anyone
- Desperate for a solution
- Certain nothing else counts besides fixing how you feel

Now, the truly amazing thing is that in spite of these "rides" that wreck everything from our health to our relationships, we still take them! Surely, if we were aware of what we were doing, nothing on Earth could convince us to hop on to what is hurting us. So, let's see what's happening to cause us to continue making the painful mistake.

An event occurs. We're not sure how to react so we naturally look for help. This is the part of the story where we put a light in the window. We know that a right response is the same as rescue. And it is. But before we know it, up pops a self that always comes complete with the appropriate thoughts and feelings to support why we should let it be in charge of the moment. Simply put, this is the dark horse and carriage, and it's there to carry us off. In the past we've always been so grateful for the arrival of that response that told us who we were and what to do that we never questioned it. But now we want to be self-ruling rather than going off on one ride after another to nowhere. We remember the warning the king gave to his son. We know that before we release ourselves into the hands of any automatically appearing rescuing agent, we must first take it into the Light in order to see who sent it.

This royal power to discern dark horses from light ones is already ours; but to wield it, there is a key, a secret step that must be taken. This higher power to choose what will carry us—and what won't—is only as powerful as our willingness to come to a special kind of psychic pause, an inner halt. By working to momentarily anchor ourselves in the present moment, we bring our own thoughts and feelings into the Light of consciousness to see them for what they are. Once again, that test is fairly clean and simple. In that moment, it's not so much going with what "feels right" as it is basing our choice in seeing what is truly *for* us; in knowing without thinking about it that no negative state wants what is right for us.

This exercise of taking a psychic pause may sound as though it would be easy, but it takes practice and persistent effort. You see, it's very tempting to just let ourselves be carried away. In fact, there's nothing to it! Then the rest of our time is spent trying to straighten out the bad rides we've taken. All this not only steals our energy but also keeps us from being someplace real. So now, we're going to take that pause before we believe that any automatic response is the right one. We're going to learn to stay awake. And this awake state is crucial, because the evil wizard is clever. He has tricks that can take a dark horse and make it look bright. For instance, haven't we all had bad spills born out of our own false sense of elation or overconfidence? And a feeling of triumph over the defeat of others can be just as punishing as a state of desolation or anger. With time, we learn to take no horse at face value. When in doubt, try to recall this axiom: *The proof of the horse is in the ride.* If the ride is punishing or meandering, we're in the wrong carriage.

Now, suppose we wake up and realize our position too late, after we've entered the wrong carriage and are already rolling along. Perhaps we see that we're being dragged along by a state of anxiety or anger. In the past, we always accepted these negativities as being appropriate reactions, but now we recognize them as being wrong for us and unnecessary. We no longer want their direction to be our own. What do we do now?

First, we shouldn't try to stop the horse. It's a waste of energy. So is trying to convince ourselves that we're not in that state, or feeling guilty about it, or to fight it in any other way. These choices are just backup dark horses! The only way out is to choose to just come wide awake to all the thoughts and feelings running through us at the moment. This conscious choice transforms us from a person who is completely identified with the runaway state into a person who is aware of it. Through that awareness, we jump out of the wild carriage back into the safety, sanity, and solid ground of the present moment.

Jumping clear of your own jumbled self takes special skills, but these come to you as you see the need for them. So, don't get discouraged. Stay off of that horse! You may fail many times before you jump clear successfully, but look at the progress we've made already. We now know that we tend to get into wrong carriages; we also know it's not necessary to do so. No runaway thought and feeling is who we really are.

Our new aim is to "look" before we leap into a relationship with any interior state that promises us safety. Each time we catch ourselves caught up in some reaction—searching desperately for a "carriage" to carry us away from the conflict we're in—we can be pretty sure that the wrong horse is on its way—that is to say, if it hasn't already arrived! But now that we can see how we've been deceived into taking these dark rides, we also know what's needed for us to choose the right carriage: start with the Light that starts things right. Here's one of the ways that you can put this new power into practice. Always remember that any thought or feeling that arrives telling you—compelling you—to hurry up and climb aboard its solution has come for only one reason: to carry you away from the Light within yourself that knows you have nothing to run from … ever.

Adapted in part from
Who Put That Stone in My Shoe?

The Power to Never Feel Powerless Again

KEY LESSON

Fear and anger—as is true of all negative states—are "undercover agents." Their "soul" task, in any moment of conflict with life, is to rush in and cover up any possible impression that would otherwise reveal we don't possess the "powers" we pretend to.

We may not like to admit it, but—in one way or another—we often feel trapped by life. If this weren't true, we wouldn't spend as much time as we do trying to escape our circumstances. The problem is we're so involved with trying to imagine and swim to our own Fantasy Island that we've never really considered this important question: What if the condition we want to escape from is only an illusion that *feels* real? How would such a realization change our lives?

We're going to look into these questions, starting with the feeling itself of being trapped. So, what do we know about it? For one thing, it is neither gender nor economically selective; everyone has a share of this unwanted state of self, regardless of his or her social status. We also know that none of us would remain feeling trapped if we really possessed the power to change our condition. Which leads us to this finding:

More times a day than we want to acknowledge, we feel *powerless*. In such moments, for whatever reason, we see our situation as being without a solution. Confusion starts coloring our considerations. Frustration grows and surrounds us, and we find ourselves imprisoned behind a wall of fearful expectations. But we need not and must not accept being sentenced to a life of such limitation. We can uncover the root of this powerless feeling—and release ourselves from it—by discovering the nature of the illusion that creates it. For most of us, the show gets started like this:

"Why did he have to do that?"—or—"Life isn't fair!"—or—"They took this away from me." Whatever the trigger may be at the moment . . . feeling powerless has a thousand reasons but, as we are going to discover, the same cause.

So, let's get started with our study by setting the record straight: whatever these "reasons," they are not the source of our pressing stress! The first thing we have to see is that these moments are events, not powers. This means they are passing conditions, not prisons. With this fact in mind, the real question we must now ask ourselves isn't "How do we regain our lost power?" but "What is it about these kinds of events that causes us to feel powerless?" Let's examine this important difference in perception. Our discoveries will help us to realize a whole new kind of power that cannot be held captive by any condition.

First, a few vital facts: The feeling of being powerless has nothing to do with what someone else did or didn't do. And the feeling of being powerless has nothing whatsoever to do with what you did or didn't do at any point in your life—regardless of your present conditions. Now let's prove these statements to ourselves by doing a little detective work.

What's the first thing we see when we hear news that runs counter to what we want? The evidence suggests we don't really "see" anything at all; instead our attention is seized, absorbed by a familiar negative reaction whose only wish is that the unwanted moment just go away. This resistance acts within and upon our consciousness as a "blinding" and binding force, so all we can "see" is our own negativity over what we wish wasn't happening! In moments like these we are literally looking at what we *don't* want to be there. Let's clarify this fascinating idea with some common examples.

- Whenever someone hurts us with a pointed remark, what we see isn't whether or not there's truth in their words; all we see is our wish they hadn't said anything at all!
- When expectations get dashed, we don't see new possibilities unfolding; all we see is the way things should have gone. We don't see *what is* with all of its positive

possibilities; instead we see only the negative ... *what is not.*

What these discoveries reveal is as startling as it is promising: the only reason we feel powerless is because we have become the captive of *a mind resisting itself,* an involuntary prisoner of a mind struggling to escape its own negative images. And there is nothing but powerlessness in this resistance, because by law whatever we resist ... persists!

There is only one way to liberate ourselves from the confines of this unconscious relationship; we need a new awareness of what it costs us to remain in its captivity. Our own honest answers to a few questions will help do just that.

- What possible good does it do to resent any moment for unfolding as it does, to wish it didn't happen? Does it change the moment in any positive way? No, it does not.
- Does our pain prove our position as being the right one? To the contrary: the more we don't want the moment in which we find ourselves, the more we lend credibility to that moment as being overpowering. This false perception then strengthens our negative sense of self as the one being overpowered by it.

We must validate for ourselves this next insight if we wish to know the freedom it foretells: whenever we find ourselves feeling like a powerless captive of some condition, it's because we grabbed on to the false power of worry, fear, anger, self-loathing, self-pity to lend us strength. You name it:

All negative states are a waste that waste our lives whenever we embrace their empty promise of empowerment.

What is real power? Here's a whole new definition for it: Real power is knowing we already possess everything we need to succeed in the moment, as we would wish it. Let's examine this important idea.

What good is any conditional power we may have—social or financial—if, when a challenging moment comes along, we can't count on that power to be there for us? We've all seen what happens when—due to "unscheduled changes"—our power source is suddenly unplugged. We either collapse into feeling powerless or start scrambling around searching for ways to regain our base of power. Regardless of our response, we remain a captive of these reactions.

Whenever you see an angry person, you are looking at someone who just found out he does not possess the power he imagined his own. All that's left in such moments is for this individual to defend his imagined loss by blaming others for it; now his false power is in being resentful. Comparing this kind of "power" to the one that follows makes our discovery clear.

Real power lifts us above challenging circumstances; it shelters us from those fears that want to drag us down into troubled thoughts about tomorrow. In a word, real power is the quiet but certain understanding that *everything that comes to us works for the good of us,* no matter what it is. How do we enter into relationship with such pure power? We begin with a startling insight:

We inhabit a world in which human beings have mistaken themselves as being powers unto themselves. The truth tells a different story: we are the instruments of these powers, high and low; and yet, our unique place in reality gives us a far greater role to play than any (one) of these archetypal forces can ever hope to know. We alone are empowered to choose— from *all* powers, potential or present—which of them we will embody and serve by expression.

Let's look closer at this core concept that is the heart of every true religion since the beginning of time.

We introduced this section with the idea that even though we often find ourselves feeling so, in truth ... there is no such thing as being powerless. We see how a person who resists life— who hates or fears unwanted changes—becomes the instrument of a power that effectively renders him powerless to do anything but struggle. But we've seen the converse as well: the one who realizes that the only power negative states have is to create the illusion of self-command enters into a relationship with another kind of power altogether. And this new awareness, like the power it grants, is failsafe.

We can practice this true, new power anytime we wish to have its strength and safety as our own. We start each time by remembering that *ours is the power to choose what we will and will not give our power to.* A short study of the following examples reveals this new and higher possibility:

- Rather than live with the pain of a thousand regrets, we can realize that no number of visits to a painful past can change it. The light of this new awareness empowers us to start over now.

- Rather than look to anxious thoughts to help us through some fearful situation, we can see that anxiety *serves fear* —so how can it free us from it? The light of this new awareness empowers us to let go of both these imposters.
- Rather than defend our mistakes by finding excuses for them, we can understand that our refusal to learn the lesson at hand ensures we will meet that lesson again, along with its misery. The light of this new awareness empowers us to accept what life would teach us, and the truth sets us free.

Can we see the difference in these three life cases? On one hand, negative states want to convince us we are powerless in the face of what frustrates us. But we have seen the truth: this false perception is actually produced by a dark state that would have us turn to it for the power we need to make things right. And now we can do something radically new: rather than give ourselves over to the habitual reaction of resisting the moment, we remember the truth that sets us free; ours is the power to live from the power of our choosing. Said slightly differently, but equally true: *We are created with the power to surrender our sense of powerlessness* and, in exchange for this sacrifice, realize a life without stress and strife.

A short review of these important ideas will help us to start practicing this new kind of power over feeling powerless.

Whenever we have a pain or a problem that seems greater than our ability to deal with it, this doesn't mean that we are really without power. These moments are "wake-up calls"—invitations to remember our relationship with an indwelling and Divine order of ourselves that is the same as our True Nature. This new action on our part, this conscious realignment born of higher self-awareness, is the same as our rescue. Our sense of being powerless is replaced by releasing the misunderstanding over who we really are. Now the words "Let go and let God" take on new meaning for us. We have come to understand what must be done in order to let the Divine Light do for us what we can't: *To know true power, we must release all claims upon it.*

The Great Gift of Being Your Self

KEY LESSON

Even as we prepare to become what we will be, what we already are both guides us now and awaits us there.

Deep within each of us lives an essential longing to be at peace in ourselves and with wherever life may take us. In a word, regardless of what's unfolding around us, we want to know that we are in the right place, at the right time, doing the right thing—and to *know* it in such a fashion that nothing can come along and convince us otherwise. But there is only one way to possess this indisputable interior confidence: such a life comes only to those who are willing to do the inner work that leads to being a true individual, what we will call being a "singularity."

It is "written" in us to be and express our individuality as surely as each petal on a rose unfolds unlike any other. But instead of this natural "flowering"—with all the fulfillment it brings to the aspiring soul—we walk the path of social convention: we think to ourselves, "What must I do to be seen as being an individual?" Then we look out into the world around us, full of people asking the same question, and find someone or something after which to fashion our individuality; then we work to "be like" whatever makes us feel that we are unlike anyone else! Our lives become imitations, and our emptiness the price of having sold ourselves for nothing.

The gift of true individuality is that it has no need to be recognized as such; it places no demands on anyone to acknowledge its unique character because its essential character is uniqueness itself. The "unessential" life is the struggle for approval, for acceptance ... always trying to get other people to confirm the image we hold of ourselves. A real life is without this stress because it is based in the expression of an individuality that needs nothing outside of itself in order to feel whole.

Can you find anything in the universe that isn't created for the specific purpose of fulfilling a task that only it can do or be? From a distant cluster of stars to a microscopic strand of our own DNA, everything is created in its essence to express what nothing else can. How can we—for whom all things created exist—be less than that?

We do not create individuality any more than a towering pine makes itself rise above all else; it is our interior right to know the integrity of singularity as each of the following key lessons points out. Study each on its own until, by its light, you can see the possibility of a new kind of freedom that takes nothing more than being true to your Self.

Adapted in part from
the audio album *Living Now*

SPECIAL KEY LESSONS IN REVIEW

1. Any concern over what others may think of you is a secret form of captivity, an unseen prison cell created by the false and painful belief that you are real—and your life worthwhile—only if others say it's so!

2. The true individual is one who doesn't need the approval of others in order to know the peace of mind he finds in being just himself.

3. If common social convention—with all is contrivance and hypocrisy—has one redeeming value, it is this: The happy day may come when we realize that our lives have been spent conversing with thieves, making plans with liars, and listening to promises of people, most of whom are incapable of a single act of integrity. This day of our awakening is the same as the delightful date of our departure from a bankrupt world filled with beggars dressed as kings and queens.

4. That we should search only our own conscience for confirmation of what is good and true is the best definition of integrity. For that which is good and true is not social in nature, but spiritual in need and in deed.

5. Psychological irritation is an indication of having been in a waking dream out of which we have been suddenly made to awaken.

Chapter 5

REALIZE THE INVISIBLE HEART OF HAPPY HUMAN RELATIONSHIPS

The Secret of Perfect Relationships

KEY LESSON

The only thing that really troubles us about others, that puts us in conflict with them, is what we would have them be!

Most of us are confused about our relationships with others; on one hand we naturally long for companionship. But, as we all know, it's not that easy. The challenge is that being around others on a continual basis seems to produce as many new pains as it solves our old problem of not wanting to go through life alone! This double-edged sword—of feeling as pleased at times as we are punished by our relationships—expresses itself in a number of ways.

For example, there is a unique contentment that comes with sharing our lives, with finding someone who understands us well enough to help us better understand ourselves. However, this same longing that enables us to share the secret recesses of our heart with another often boomerangs back on us. Who hasn't been knocked flat when a privately disclosed weakness— told to one we love—is thrown back in our face? And what about when we go to a friend seeking consolation about our condition only to receive what feels like condemnation?

Along similar lines, perhaps we go to someone hoping to get her on our side of a fight with friends or family. But instead of agreeing with our side, she insists it is we who are mistaken and who must change our view. Ouch! In an instant, the ranks of our enemies swell along with our suffering. Yet again we feel betrayed. 'Round and 'round we go seeking solace, only to feel isolated because "no one understands us."

Our real problem with others isn't that they won't or can't give to us what we want from them. As we're about to discover, the true seed of discontent lies deeper than this. The short writing you're about to read is intended to help shed light on the real source of our unrest in our relationships.

The less we learn to long for—or depend upon—
Special understanding from others,
The less we will suffer for not receiving this.

The less we suffer over what others
Seem incapable of giving to us,
The less unhappy will we find ourselves
In these unanswered moments of our lives
Spent in the company of friends and foes alike.

The less pain we have over what life appears to deny us,
The more at peace we naturally become with ourselves.

The more of this serenity we grow to know within ourselves,
The easier it becomes for us to give to others
This harmony founded in our New Understanding.

Whenever we give others this new order of Understanding
Without asking for anything in return,
Those we greet with this Gift are silently touched;
They are moved
By this willingness to put their concerns before our own.
And it is this one action that awakens in them . . .
Their sleeping need to respond in kind.

Happiness is the wholeness found in conscious kindness.
This is the secret of perfect relationships.

Give Yourself What You Really Want

KEY LESSON

Why is it that we so seldom remember to help another at
the cost of ourselves, and yet find it so hard to forget those
who fail to remember us in our hour of need?

We have been looking at how and why our relationships with
one another are often a source of distress. And, as we have
seen—speaking in general terms—most of the conflict we experience with others has to do with some form of consideration
that we feel they are not giving to us. We often suffer from
thoughts like these: "She is not being respectful enough." "He is
not as kind as I want him to be." "They just don't care as deeply
as I do." However, if we will be courageous enough to see the
truth of the next insight—admit its finding into our heart and

mind—something new and wonderful can happen within us: we can release ourselves from this dissatisfaction we feel in our relationships with others, along with the conflict it generates between us.

Many times the very thing we want from those we are with— for example, respect, patience, or a just little tenderness—is the very thing that we ourselves either lack at the moment or otherwise are somehow withholding from them.

The catch here is that we are mostly clueless about our own impoverished condition in these moments because quietly tucked away in the depths of us are certain clever "self-concealing devices." The continuing presence of these unconscious parts of us ensures we never realize that *it is we who run in debt* because of how quickly they point out the inadequacies of those they judge. Each time our attention is successfully diverted in this way, here's what unfolds: Not only are we kept from coming awake to ourselves, but in this engineered spiritual sleep we are rendered unable to realize that the very quality we judge as missing in the person before us is actually lacking in ourselves!

Some needed inner light reveals the truth of our actual condition. We almost always place certain character demands upon others, but rarely see that the part of us making these demands is without the very substance it cries out as missing in them. No wonder the cycle of human disharmony rolls on as it does; this spiritual sleep is not just the breeding ground of the contempt we feel for the insensitivity of others, it is the *source* of it!

What's to be done? How can we transform ourselves and, at the same time, serve as agents for change in the lives of all those we meet along the Way? Let's see. Please consider the following example through whatever personal experience of your own best applies; it's intended to help make a special point that can only be driven home by your willingness to discover its subtle lesson.

When, in our love for the Divine—either through prayer, contemplation, or meditation—we give to that Light our praise or adoration—we are in fact graced by that Life in proportion to the amount of love we find in our hearts to offer It. The true Friends of God have always known this law of reciprocal Divine Love. In other words, whatever we give our love to gives us that love back according to the extent of our giving. The true pleasure of *anything* we practice for our love of it—gardening, golf, cooking, music, or whatever—*is the love we have for that same action.*

Now, with this idea in mind, let's apply it to our need to open our hearts and stop judging others for what we see as missing in them. Here is the great principle that makes possible true harmony between all human beings: *Giving to others what we ask from them is how we receive what we wish.*

This spiritual principle deserves our consideration, so let's take a close look at it through the eyes of our everyday experience with others. How many of us feel that the "others" in our life—particularly those people we are around every day, whether at home or at work—just don't treat us as we deserve? Again, perhaps not all of the time, most of us feel slighted in our relationships. But how many of us can honestly say that we offer to our friends and fellows what we want from them?

Generally we extend olive branches and our considerate sympathies to those who we think can serve us, and rarely do we serve those who we are convinced have nothing we want. And yet we still want their respect, kindness, or consideration. With this in mind, let's return to the guiding principle for this section: *We must learn to give to others what we hope to get from them.* Here now are a few simple suggestions for how we can get started with enacting our new understanding.

- Before we ask for someone's attention, let us first lend that person our own.
- Before we look to him or her for an act of consideration, let us offer one from ourselves.
- If we wish for kindness, let it begin with our own. Otherwise all we give each other are unconscious demands followed by judgment and disappointment.

We must learn to take the true conscious initiative with each other and then—based in our understanding of this great spiritual law that governs harmonious relationships—make the effort to be to others what we wish them to be for us. Here is a special exercise that can help us create more harmonious human relationships.

We all know what it's like to find ourselves unhappy and in conflict with someone who just isn't giving us what we want or need from him or her. Whenever this happens, we usually find fault with these people, judge them as being inadequate, and from these findings blame them for the negativity we now feel toward them. But how many of us are awake enough to offer these same people what we have asked them to give us—before we ask them for it?

Even to attempt the following practice will reveal more to you about yourself than reading a thousand books on spiritual realization. To begin with, as we discussed earlier, we usually demand from others those interior qualities that we are in short supply of ourselves. For instance, it is impatience that leaps to judge impatience. Unkindness finds others unkind—and tells them so in no uncertain terms. Arrogance despises pride and makes sure that the proud know they are dreaming of unreal heights. On and on churns this cycle of disharmony until we go to work on ourselves, implementing the kind of true self-transforming principles that follow.

Whatever it may be that we find wanting in someone else, we must learn what it means to give that very thing to him or her. *What we would have from others, or have them be toward us, we must provide or be ourselves.*

For instance, if we really want the person we are with to be open with us, we must first open up ourselves. When we know we tend to be critical of others because they don't show us the respect we would have, we must show these same people the respect we want.

Now, add to these thoughts this last idea: Sometimes we want from others what they just don't have within themselves to give. We make demands, for instance, that someone understand us when—at this stage in his or her development—there's no way on Earth that could happen. But wanting what we want *when we want it* leaves no room in us for compassionate understanding. We show our weariness with such "weakness" in others through impatience or other condescending acts. This behavior on our part only convinces the person in question of his own shortcomings. What can we do instead?

Give to him or to her what we have of ourselves instead of taking away what little these individuals have in themselves. To give the fruit of such a conscious interior labor is to receive the goodness we ask for.

This exercise to help awaken our sleeping conscience takes a great deal of attention and, more importantly, a great deal of being weary with finding everyone around us not as good as ourselves. Nevertheless, real spiritual growth—true self-transformation—depends upon what we are willing to give, and not upon what we feel we are owed.

Put these higher ideas to work in all your affairs with others. You will be shocked, amazed, and highly encouraged by your discoveries, but, most important of all, here's what you'll find: instead of being the exception to the rule, harmonious relationships with others will be your daily reality. Everything is better and brighter everywhere in the world around you because of the new Light of self-understanding now living within you.

Take the First Step to True Independence

KEY LESSON

We can spend our time struggling, in vain, to make others into what we want them to be, or we can see the inherent flaw in thinking this way and—rather than trying to change others to suit our needs—see through the false idea that someone else can make us whole.

Real self-independence is the fruit of an awakened inner life. And just as fruit on a tree must develop into fullness following a certain order of natural events, so too is there a natural order to interior discovery that leads up to winning your own life and living it as you please.

Every step along the way to this higher independent life is both the challenge and the reward. The challenge is always in how dark and uncertain the next step appears to be; and the reward, after you take the step, is the sweet and relief-filled discovery that who you really are cannot fall! In this way, step by step, you can realize the natural independence of your own True Self.

However, as with any climb to a loftier view, there are always those spots that are more difficult than others to negotiate. The more light we can shed on these psychological outcrops that obscure our vision, the smoother our upward journey will be. Remember, Truth will never lead you to an impasse. If it ever seems that way, it is only because you are needlessly trying to take something along with you that can't be part of the higher life that awaits you just ahead. So let go. You will rise to the next step effortlessly.

One of the major obstacles in the climb to self-independence, the point at which many students falter and so fail to take the next important step upward, is in their reluctance to see that the human condition is far worse off than imagined. You must be different. As you are about to see, only your unwavering insight into the low life-level of society—including its political and religious leaders—can bring into play the new energies you need to transform yourself into a truly independent person. This higher kind of independence is the only ground from which can grow the kindness and strength one needs in order to have authentically healthy relationships with others.

So you must never hesitate to see through people, nor should you ever feel guilty for what your awakening perception reveals to you about them. This guilty feeling, as if you've done something bad by seeing badness in others, is a trick of the false self. It needs to keep you believing in others so that later on you can feel stressed and betrayed when they fail to live up to your expectations.

In his stunning little book *50 Ways to See Through People,* Vernon Howard explains exactly why we must never feel bad about seeing badness.

> Some students of human nature are reluctant about exposing falseness and weakness in others. They think they should not see so much badness. The opposite is right. You should and must know all about hurtful human behavior, for only exposure of the wrong can invite the right. The real peril is to not see things as they are, for delusion is dangerous to the deluded. Believing that a shark is a dolphin is both foolish and unnecessary. When a wise man sees a shark he knows it is a shark. Since when is it wrong to see right?

So it is both wise and profitable to collect facts about the weakness of human nature. Indeed, if our search for true independence is to have a happy ending, we must learn not only to welcome these temporarily shocking insights, but we must gather ourselves up and ask to see more. The Truth will oblige.

Here are three friendly facts to help us let go and grow more spiritually independent.

1. No matter how it may appear on the surface of human events, self-interest governs individuals.

2. You can only depend on others for as long as it pays them to tolerate your dependence.

3. Even the typical display of human kindness or benevolence comes not from that person's compassionate nature but from his unconscious desire to enrich himself with the intoxicating feelings of being a good person. Forget to thank him or acknowledge his generosity, and watch how quickly his goodness turns into repressed resentment or outward indignation.

These facts are not negative. What is negative is to hide from ourselves that we have not only been betrayed by others, but that we have ourselves played the same regretful role at some point in our lives. The evidence is overwhelming.

Depending on others for a sense of psychological well-being is an accident waiting to happen. In any relationship where we depend on our partner to be our "parachute," and the other accepts this role, both will fall to the ground. You do not have to live with this kind of fear for one more moment.

Give yourself permission to see the whole truth about human nature and its affairs; in turn, the Truth will show you something about yourself that will lift you high above any of your present painful concerns. So don't be afraid to come to the disturbing but wonderful understanding that there is no one for you to count on—because there isn't—*at least not where you have been looking.* This gradual realization of your true and present position in life is actually a step up that only feels, temporarily, like a step down. And the only reason it feels like this is that, unknown to yourself, you have been living with the self-limiting belief that one day someone will give you what you haven't been able to give to yourself: true independence. Well, the wait is over, and so is the fear.

There is a secret and miraculous part of yourself that only reveals itself when you are willing to stand in the light of the truth about yourself and others. Welcome this light and you will discover that a wise and uncompromised inner strength is patiently waiting for you to fulfill the laws that govern its entrance into your life.

Adapted in part from The Secret of Letting Go

New Keys for Living in Conscious Harmony

KEY LESSON

To know the real pleasure of a relationship with any other person requires no thought on our part. On the other hand, thoughtlessness wrecks any relationship into which it rears its ugly head.

Deep spiritual work reveals the truth that hellish things on Earth manifest as they do because their dark cause dwells hidden somewhere in us. We are about to look into this interior abyss and shine into its unseen corners a beautiful Light of understanding. We will illuminate the center of the unconscious "earth" within us where dark forces are always celebrating some victory over unsuspecting human beings.

Imagine the chief devil calling together every possible evil entity that is in range of his magnetic voice and saying, "How can we interfere up there in the world that dwells between ours and the Light we despise? What can we do to further deceive human beings? We must keep them living in the dark, unaware of the Light that wants to release them from our influence. I want something so evil, so sinister, that no one will know what happened. Who's got a good idea?"

That instant the flames of all the little imps gathered there in the smoldering dark go dim; they're afraid of their leader, who will fry them for failing. A day later, as planned, they all return with a few ideas, although nothing spectacular. Then, out of nowhere, one tiny imp hops on the shoulder of the chief devil and whispers something in his ear. A second later, and—*kaboom!*—flames shoot out of every pore of the chief devil as he shouts, "Ah! I have the plan in hand!"

He looks around at all of his lieutenants, each of whom is assigned to certain individuals on Earth, and gleefully instructs them: "I want you to go up there and slowly spread among the sleeping masses the idea of 'tolerance.' Do whatever it takes to succeed. Convince them that this idea is their own, and that they should start teaching that learning to tolerate each other is the same as loving one another. Oh yes! This is my best deception yet! It's a real killer!"

We have had sown into our minds a certain social contrivance, a convenient mechanical reaction called "tolerating" those people who do not meet our approval. We tolerate those who don't please us or who rub us the wrong way. And we believe that our ability to tolerate another individual is the same as learning to live in harmony with him or her. Nothing could be further from the truth.

It is through just such a deception that human beings have almost lost the possibility of being able to see how true love is being choked out of us and off this planet. As surely as there are objects that choke the throat, there are false beliefs and the actions they enable that choke the soul. Now let's examine what's behind this false idea of tolerating others, and learn what it will take to remove this unnatural obstruction.

We must begin by recognizing the following truth: *All forms of tolerance have their root in one form or another of resistance,* a fact that should make the next truth obvious to us: *We cannot resist something, be negative toward it, and be in a loving relationship with it at the same time.*

Here's what this means practically speaking: when we unconsciously think to ourselves, "I will tolerate this person; I will put up with his dark manifestation, but only because I don't want anyone to see just how negative he makes me"—then what has happened to us? We come to think of ourselves as being "loving" because we repress our wish to lash out at whoever disturbs us.

Government and social institutions heavily promote this idea of tolerance to maintain the illusion of a progressive, evolving society; but to love one another has absolutely nothing whatsoever to do with harboring resistance while calling it acceptance. Resistance isolates, separates, and chokes. Love embraces, welcomes, and breathes freely. But there is more yet to see here, if we will.

The whole notion of this order of tolerance is rooted in the idea of superiority, as only a superior person tolerates an inferior human being. When we are with someone, and we must "tolerate" him or her, we are in a state of secret self-love that keeps itself in place by having that which it quietly denigrates. But this unconscious state of self is only half the limitation.

Unconscious self-superiority keeps itself in place through a process of resisting what it imagines it isn't like, but by the fact of the negative reaction proves its unseen likeness. Shakespeare said, "Methinks thou dost protest too much," because he was pointing out that what we most strongly deny in another is what we unconsciously recognize in ourselves.

The first step in harmonious relationships is simple: We need only realize the spiritual truth that we cannot meet someone whom we are not like in some way, even if we don't actively express what we don't like seeing in him or her. The deception is that we're sure we're unlike everyone except for those who match the images we have of ourselves. And so it goes that we live from—see our lives through the eyes of a certain false sense of "I" that always resists anyone seen as being "not like I am." But love cannot grow where resistance rules.

We have not been given this precious life in order to go through it resisting everything that doesn't suit us; rather we are created to grow through whatever we meet along the way. Resistance devitalizes the possibility of our spiritual development, rendering useless the conditions in our lives that we are given in order to rise above them. When we resist what others show us about ourselves, we close the door on the possibility of transcending *the undiscovered parts of us* that are troubled by them. Freedom is not found by avoiding what disturbs us, but by illuminating—realizing and releasing—whatever may dwell in the dark of us that can be disturbed.

The human being is created to develop in the "likeness" of that marvelous Intelligence that made us. This Divine Intelligence didn't create anything that it fears or hates. It's a ridiculous thought to walk around and believe (as we all do because of the strong sense of self that it produces) that another person is our enemy simply because we feel enmity for him or her.

Now, just so we're clear on this, there are plenty of unpleasant people. Our world is packed with them! But, given the negative effect of resenting others, and the fact that (for now) all we know to do about those who disturb us is to resist them, could it be that when it comes to our human relationships we have been blinded to one of the main reasons for them? The answer is "Yes."

Just as the wind moves through a tree and carries its pollen to the blossoms of another tree, our relationships are intended to help "pollinate" the soul so that true understanding of why we are here on Earth can flower within it. We grow through our relationships with life, which means that through them we are shown possibilities about ourselves we never knew existed. To exclude any of these discoveries is to deny ourselves the truth of ourselves, something the Truth within us would never do. This understanding makes something else abundantly clear:

This idea of tolerating human beings can't possibly be the seed of something celestial. This part of us that has become a master of tolerating those whom we can't stand has come to be as strong and prevalent as it is because of how superior it makes us feel when we are around them. This unconscious self-righteousness is not an act of love but a form of hatred; it is a weakness.

Now, here's a special spiritual exercise designed to develop harmonious human relationships. Just as we can be taught the Heimlich maneuver—a swift action that can be taken to dislodge what is choking the body—we can learn a spiritual maneuver that we may call upon every day, as often as it is necessary, to help us dislodge something that is presently choking our soul. The point of this exercise and the new understanding it reveals is to help us get past the unconscious thinking that we can do something against ourselves and expect a positive outcome.

This exercise is called the "You-I Maneuver." You can work with it every moment of the day, whether you're with people or you're sitting alone and thinking about someone. To employ this maneuver effectively, you will need to be as sensitive in your interactions with other people as a spider web is to the slightest breeze; your True Nature is just that responsive. Much as a crystal-clear lake reflects the overhead sky, any state of energy we encounter resonates with its counterpart within us. In that same instant, if we are willing, we may share in that consciousness.

And there is no limit to this gift except for what we unknowingly throw away through acts of unconscious resistance to what we are being shown.

When we're around other people, and have a negative reaction toward them, we don't realize that some form of resistance already rules the moment. Feeling the need to tolerate someone couldn't appear within us unless something in us did not want to be around someone "like that." As the intensity of this unconscious resistance rises, it takes the shape of a further negative reaction toward that "offending" person. Key to this exercise is to understand that this reaction always begins with the pejorative word *you*—as in "You are this," or "You are that." There is an instant sense of separation between one's Self and the person one is with. Further strengthening this false sense of "I" are waves of negative thoughts that ensure our "finding." Now it is certain: we know who is at fault for the conflict we feel. But now we are beginning to know better than to blame another for the negative states revealed in us.

So in this same moment, when we look at that person and sense in us the formation of this derogatory "you" starting to take shape, we are going to add the word "I" to that same "you." Now we're going to hold in our mind and heart the idea of "You-I." For instance, suppose we're resisting someone because he or she is always in a rush. Instead of just going along with being ruled by the usual negative reaction, we choose another road. *We realize our psychic similarity instead of separating ourselves by it.* This new understanding is expressed something like this: "You ... I have seen the exact same character in me." For instance if an angry person comes to us, instead of tolerating his or her negative state, we work with this new maneuver through this silent realization: "You ... I have seen the exact same anger in me."

This inner exercise is good for any negative reaction we may have toward the unwanted manifestations of others. It disarms the lie of the "superior" self by effectively canceling its corrupting power to produce the illusion that we are different from the people we tolerate. And in the collapse of that opposite, love and compassion are born: "I can no longer treat you as someone to be tolerated; I realize the fact that you and I really are neighbors because we share a common burden: the need to discover the truth of ourselves through one another."

Here is a summary of the exercise called the "You-I Maneuver." We need a new intention in all of our relationships, something like this: "I will not suffer you; instead I will work to be increasingly conscious *of us,* suffering what I must for the sake of both of us. I will not cast you out as being something inferior to myself; I will not do that because I can't recognize in you anything as being an inferior condition in you unless I have it in myself."

Our work, if we're willing, is to catch that surging separation called "You are different from me." And then, in that same moment, to apply our new understanding that cancels this unconscious act of resistance. Instead, we embrace the realization that "you" and "I" are both exposed in this God-given moment that God meant for the purpose of transcending ourselves.

Remember that "tolerance" is a lie because it produces a "me" that is always apart from what I am tolerating. There cannot be love where there is separation.

Work at the "You-I Maneuver." Learn to watch this low-level self that is trying to destroy the possibility of love awakening within you. Risk leaving yourself open by refusing to identify with the parts of yourself that would have you believe that resisting life can lead to being embraced by it. Do the inner work it takes to make this exercise personally meaningful, and you will understand the greatest secret on Earth: everyone on it has a gift just for you—if only you will take it.

Evolution through Revolution: Sowing the Seeds of Peace

KEY LESSON

Any burden shared isn't just half the burden— but a burden made lighter for all who agree to carry it; the unthinkable truth is that if everyone agreed to carry just a little more, everyone would carry a little less.

If only we would cease giving others
Reasons to resist our presence,
Bear ourselves
With what we burden them,
Leaving no reason for blame ...

Then ... that great silent rage
Hidden in the human heart
Would have to be seen for what it is:
Violence looking for a war.

Such a discovery would awaken
Within the discerning soul

The immediate, most intimate need
To be the embodiment of peace.

This new need—born of seeing
Is the seed of true revolution.

All relationships suffer when stagnation sets in; whether in a pond or in our personal dealings with others, everything must be continually refreshed in order to realize its true potential. For us this means each reappearance of some old resentment, fear, or regret chokes the life out of our chance to love one another, which is our spiritual responsibility. What's so hard for us to understand is that the *real* reason these old painful patterns go on as they do isn't because other people don't change. The truth tells a very different story if we will dare to listen.

Here's why we continue to run through unwanted patterns in our relationships with others: our continual attempts to resolve the pain within us—*by holding others accountable for it*—has utterly failed.

Any new course of action we arrive at by considering what's wrong with someone else transforms nothing other than the way we will again have to suffer that relationship. Trying to resolve our problems this way is like looking out at a field we have planted on our own property and wishing, every day, something other than what grows there would take hold and flower. If we wish to have true harmonious relationships with others, then *it is we who must change.* We must assume responsibility for what our relationships reveal to us about us, and then do the interior work it takes to plant the seeds of a new Self.

Since before records were made of their teachings, the wise ones have all taught this same great lesson: *We reap what we sow.* In these so-called progressive times, this all but forgotten principle is as simple as it is prophetic. What we are inwardly is what we get. Our experience of life, moment to moment, is a reflection of our character that those same moments reveal. Share this simple fact with someone who hates his life, and he will despise you for the truth you tell him about why he feels as he does!

Everywhere we look, people are concerned with essentially one thing: getting what they want, when they want it, and as fast as possible. The fires that fuel their appetite for this envisioned success create so much smoke that they lose sight of the fact that all they reap for their insistent sowing are the cold ashes of regret raked out of broken relationships.

If we are ever to realize the integrity and consistent kindness of our True Self, if we long to know something of heaven while we live on Earth, then we must sow the seeds that bring that higher life into fruition. One cannot expect to reap what one does not sow; and merely hoping for a higher life is not sowing true spiritual seeds, any more than climbing an imagined mountain is the same as reaching its top.

To sow spiritual seeds means that we do spiritual work. Spiritual work is always interior work first, even if, as a matter of course, this work becomes manifest through exterior action. What is this interior work by which we sow the seeds of the celestial within us? The following four ways to sow the seeds of a higher relationship with life are taken from my book, *Let Go and Live in the Now.*

1. We must work to not burden others or ourselves with past regrets, disappointments, or fearful future visions, even as we learn to ask Truth for more insight into those unseen aspects of our present nature that are reaping their regrets even as they sow more of the same dark seeds.

2. We must learn to sit quietly with ourselves and wait patiently for the Light of God's peace to replace those dark, noisy thoughts and feelings telling us that we have too much old baggage to make the journey home. Each time we sow these seeds through some quiet meditation, we reap the strength that comes from realizing that this silence that comes to us is our true home.

3. We must deliberately remember our intention to start our whole life over every moment we awaken to find ourselves reliving some past conflict. To cultivate this refreshed outlook, born of remembering that our true life is always new in the Now, is to let go of who we have been and to begin reaping a life free of anger and fear.

4. We must learn to look our fears, weariness, and anxiety directly in the eye, and instead of seeing what is

impossible according to their view of life, sow the seeds of a new Self by daring to doubt their dark view of things. Our refusal to identify with self-limiting negative states reaps us the reward of rising above their inherent limitations.

It is not enough to just sow seeds in this physical life, that is, to struggle for or make millions, invent the greatest gizmo ever, or become the "who's who" of some social registry; for regardless of how sublime these intentions first seem, and even if their seeds should grow and flourish, they can only grow into forms that pass and fall in time.

If our wish is for a life that is whole and loving, one that is filled with new light, then we must sow these eternal seeds within ourselves; that is our work. Make your own list of ways to work at sowing the seeds of the higher life. Set yourself to the task of being an inwardly awake person and watch how you begin to reap the awareness that makes all things possible.

Adapted in part from Let Go and Live in the Now

SPECIAL KEY LESSONS IN REVIEW

1. The pretense of kindness, of being loving, does not make those qualities real in us any more than an actor who plays the role of a talking tree in a play by Shakespeare is endowed with the strength of an oak!

2. It is not our duty to suffer over what will be or won't be—to live with painful regret or guilt over what was or wasn't. Our sole task is to be responsible for what is—and to allow this relationship with life to produce what it will. There may or may not be suffering in this order of responsibility, but, if there is, it will be transformational as opposed to self-tormenting—which is the negative effect of every act born of assuming some false responsibility.

3. Deriving our sense of self by identifying with the dilemma of another is like going to a tailor for a new suit and leaving the shop dressed in the clothes we were wearing when we walked in!

4. Learn never to blame another for the pain you feel, nor to complain about anything that life brings to your door; but this doesn't mean to be accepting of those who would see you ache, nor should you be apathetic in the face of anything that challenges your hopes and aspirations.

5. One reason that judging others so appeals to the level of self that sits in such judgment of them ... is that the comfort found in sentencing others for their "defects" serves to convince us of our perfection.

Chapter 6

BEING AT PEACE WITH
YOURSELF

The Amazing Power of a Quiet Mind

KEY LESSON

Thinking can no more produce true peace of mind than throwing a stone into the center of a pond has the power to quiet its ripples.

Day in and day out, our minds are swamped—socially, culturally, economically—with new ideas, fail-proof programs, promises of special places ... things that, if we could only acquire them, would quiet our restless minds and hearts. So it goes that most of us are always running after something to quiet that nagging sense of feeling as though we're incomplete. But repeated experience indicates this race has no finish line; all we reach is one more starting place, another task to complete before we can rest. Here's the surprising reason why we've been running, but getting nowhere fast: *we are not created to fulfill ourselves.* To understand how we became convinced otherwise is the first step in winning the lasting sense of attainment we seek. This brings us, once again, to the importance of discovering the truth about our present level of being, as the following makes evident.

The mind asleep to itself is a "divided" mind. Most of us already know something about this strange state of ourselves. One part of us wants what another part of us feels guilty about wanting; or we can't stop thinking about something that we hoped—by coming to possess it—would grant us peace. But, as we are about to discover, this divided mind of ours is even more devious than we suspect. Your work to understand the following idea is worth its weight in gold.

This divided mind believes that the pleasure it derives from what it imagines is *the same as the reality* of what it has just imagined. This is like believing that the powerful feeling you get from watching an eagle in flight is the same as your ability to fly. Such a mind "sees" a possession or power it wants, and experiences in that moment *what it gives itself to feel* about that thing. Then this same mind wants to own whatever it has imagined in order to possess the pleasure it associates with that object.

Of course there's only one problem with this process: both the object imagined and the "self" pleased by it are illusions—as is soon discovered when the mind can no longer sustain its own self-induced sensation. So, the feeling is real. But its cause is a creation of a mind that first stimulates itself and then wants to own what it has imagined. That's how it is; we are born into this world with this level of mind as our first guide.

Our journey into becoming fully identified with this divided mind begins as infants in our cribs. When something (we didn't even know what it was) bothered us, all we had to do was cry out. Then, as if out of nowhere, something good magically appeared in our mouth ... a pacifier, a bottle, some chocolate! Heaven was ours! It was that simple. And, much as is true in the animal kingdom, we learned that our instinctual cry brings us what will protect us or give us what we need to end our discomfort. And so we were taught—conditioned—from the very beginning: we need only squirm, scream, or smile sweetly long enough to receive something that pleases us. But, there's trouble in toddler's paradise! We have to grow up!

As we grow older, little by little we start to realize that we can't always cry out and have something put in our mouth! Society says, "You're too big for that now." So now we need something new to chew on. But that's no problem for us. The same divided mind—that learned to cry out to satisfy itself—evolves further. It discovers how to create for itself what it needs. Only now it's no longer just food of a physical nature that it craves. Our emerging need is for "food" of a psychological nature; we want self-comforting thoughts and feelings, and we look to receive the same from others or we produce them for ourselves. Name your need: daydreams, confirmation of some flattering image, having others to blame, future plans to escape present problems, and ten thousand other ways to "empower" yourself.

From simple immature beginnings, when the mind instinctually seeks what will satisfy it, the activity of this divided mind slowly evolves into more subtle forms of psychological sophistry until, without knowing it, *we become image eaters*—feeding ourselves with passing sensations produced by an imaginary self. Let's examine how this strange progression has imprisoned us without our even knowing it.

Whenever in our mind's eye we see "him," "her," "this," or "that" as being the remedy for the pain we're in—and feel that sense of relief for our conclusion—we see nothing wrong with our solution. After all, the disturbance is abated for the moment; we're not crying out any more! But what we don't see is that *our conception is a deception;* what we've imagined to please ourselves with is as unreal as is the self that it temporarily satisfies. Within these images produced by the mind there is no power to transcend, no real nourishment to help us grow, and never any true respite from our problems. Nothing that thought can create from itself can liberate or heal itself. *No divided mind can give itself the wholeness it seeks.* We must seek elsewhere!

As paradoxical as it seems, the reason most of us find no lasting peace in life is because our mind is forever trying to find something *outside* itself in which it can rest. This condition is not unlike the little fish that, unhappy with just swimming around, went in search of water—its hope being that if it could find what it was looking for, then it would also find what was missing from its life. This story helps us to see what our present level of mind cannot perceive:

We *already* live in the deep, silent, and restful "waters" of the present moment, and yet ... we don't know its abiding fulfillment. We can't find the unlimited freedom for which we search because each time the divided mind tells us where to look for it we become, in that instant, a captive of thought, a virtual prisoner of promise.

True peace doesn't exist outside of the *now* from out of which it is always unfolding. Our spiritual challenge—the "problem" before us—is that the true present moment cannot be known by thought because *now* is not an idea. It is a living presence that cannot be grasped any more than sunlight can be bottled. Nothing exists outside of the present moment to hold it, let alone possess the feeling of its inexpressible power.

You may be wondering, "If I don't take action to fulfill myself, to end this sense of emptiness, what will become of me? There must be something I can do to realize the wholeness for which my heart longs."

The answer to this question is, "Yes, there is a way," but the true power of peace is not found in a "place" of any kind, which is why it always eludes our search. If we are ever to attain the fulfillment of ourselves, with its attending freedom, then we need to see for ourselves what is unthinkable to our present level of mind: *self-wholeness appears by itself within us once we stop searching for it.* The next few insights taken from *Let Go and Live in the Now* help illustrate the beauty of this timeless truth.

Much in the same way as a sun-baked field of wildflowers has as its only balm the spring rains, so, too, does each season of our emptiness have but one true solution: the stirring touch of that celestial Life that seeded us with this incomplete sense of ourselves in the first place. Why are we created to experience such a seemingly bottomless emptiness in the center of ourselves? Because in coming to know this dark half of the Living Light's great unseen life, we might—of our own free will—learn to quench our thirst and fill ourselves with those life-giving waters that are ever streaming out of its eternal source.

Our True Self is, in part, a secret field where a never-ending cycle of ebb and flow plays itself out in passing expressions of alternating fullness and emptiness, much as runoff winter waters from great mountains rush down to fill valley lakes parched by the passage of summer.

But the greater part of our Original Self is to these mountains and their valley lakes as is the whole of that countryside in which these same landmarks dwell, for even though the round of seasons comes and goes, causing endless change within it, nothing really changes about it. Our True Nature lives in the ever-changing, yet never-changing now—that vast country of higher consciousness wherein we are empowered to welcome all forms of fullness and emptiness as our friends, instead of mistaking ourselves a friend of one and foe of the other.

If we would awaken to a conscious relationship with these ever-flowing forces that are the lifeblood of our True Nature, and if we are to realize that this awareness alone can free us of our fear of being empty, then what is asked of us becomes clear: we must stop trying to create conditions for ourselves through which we hope to escape the fear of our own emptiness. We must willingly slip into these seemingly dark waters of ourselves, where, if we will wait there quietly enough, we will awaken to find ourselves in the higher atmosphere of a new world.

For our spiritual daring, we will gain an intimate knowledge of these invisible eternal forces at work within us; one emptying us, even as another moves into its place to fill that open space with its new and unmistakable presence. If these words sound promising, it's because they are. As this priceless self-knowledge born of higher self-awareness grows in us, we will realize that the freedom we seek is found everywhere and all at once. We will no longer fear the end of things because at last we have seen that within ourselves, the truth of who we really are is the beginning of all things.

The Magic of a Meditative Life

KEY LESSON

When, before our inner eyes, we always have someplace better to be, or that feeling we must make something more of ourselves, we miss seeing two great truths: First, all imagined destinations are dreams whose promised fulfillment fades the nearer we draw to them ... and second, that where and who we are in each moment is a field of possibilities whose riches are not only immediate, but everlasting.

In one way, it's hard to say what has happened to the health of our world and the people upon it—not that suitable terms don't exist. The problem is that whatever picture one paints with words, it points only to a single part of the story, and we're left with an incomplete understanding of the situation. History, along with personal experience, proves that whenever our understanding of a problem is incomplete, its effect is to breed conflict. Then, blame becomes the solution, and inevitably war breaks out—first on a personal and then on a planetary level.

This global digression is evident in the deteriorating conditions taking place around us. Everywhere we see the gradual loss of even common kindness amongst ourselves; we watch as social, economic, and environmental problems steadily worsen because of our refusal to deal with them.

What we don't see is that all these issues have a common root: we have all but forgotten the purpose of our being on Earth. We have lost not only the way but also the will to know the truth of ourselves. And, out of this incomplete understanding of ourselves grows a slowly deepening state of spiritual sleep, not unlike a ball bouncing down a set of steps: false purposes produce false desires; false desires cannot be satisfied. The ensuing sense of limitation creates greed, from whose suffering no one escapes, including those who have amassed the most of our world's goods.

What can be done about this? In truth, much; but we must be wise. We need to realize that what needs to be changed begins with us, as individuals. In short, *we must stop trying to change the world we see, and begin the inner work of changing the way in which we see the world.* A change needs to take place at the very core of our nature, one that affects the way in which we relate to life.

This transformation of our interior person does not take place by a simple change in the way we think. Our perception itself must be "reborn"—as every other solution to our suffering has failed to provide lasting results. It's clear: we will not be able to think our way out of the prison that our thinking has produced. Besides, thought is basically the servant of desire, created by it over millennia to facilitate the mind's need to recognize and describe the sensory world it perceives. As such, *thought is powerless to change the content of itself, let alone the reality that it reflects upon.* Something new needs to be awakened within us that isn't habituated and that can't be conditioned. But is there such a vital and active intelligence that holds no limiting allegiance to creed, belief, or cultural form? Is there a living wisdom that serves only the wholeness from out of which it is born? As we shall see, there is.

The Presence to Be in the Present Moment

One key lesson to consider is this: *our experience of life*—how we feel in any given moment—*is the direct expression of what we are in relationship with in that moment.* Most of us spend our moments trying to keep our heads above what we perceive as the "waters" of life's unending waves: the many social, cultural, and economic uncertainties that are part of everyday life. Yet, our struggle to stay afloat is due to a fundamental misunderstanding: we are trying to think our way into a world without waves; we imagine, and so believe, that we can create a world for ourselves that is free of disturbances.

The problem is this: *no such realm exists as we imagine it.*

The only world not in conflict with constant change is the present moment *whose timeless nature is both the medium of change as well as the endless changing taking place within it.* Let's use a common image familiar to all of us to help illustrate this spiritual principle: the ocean never resists its own waves. Its "life" is inclusive of any and all of its manifestations, so it is never at war with itself—or—with whatever may be moving through or upon itself.

We have all felt the calming effect of this kind of unity when we stand on the ocean's shore and gaze out on its endless waters. In moments like these our relationship with the ocean is a meditative one; the mind naturally quiets down in the presence of immensity beyond the scope of its thought to contain it. So, the relationship between the ocean and our awareness of it creates a living meditation. Peace prevails. We know a pleasure that is one with the power of that moment in which we watch the ocean's waves move through us.

Most of us hold the unquestioned belief that our hearts and minds are at peace before one of life's "waves" washes in to disturb us. But if we take away the prejudice of self-pleasing images, and add the ease with which we are disturbed by unwanted moments, we have good cause to suspect something entirely different about ourselves. Could a truer view of what takes place in such time of trouble look something like this? One of life's many unpredictable waves rolls in, rocks our bed of dreams, and we get shaken awake!

One thing should be obvious to us: no one can be free who blames his or her unsettled stressful state on life's unwanted events. Said a bit differently, how can we ever hope to be at peace with life if we fear, at any moment, that it may wash away our contentment? And that's the point: until we understand how the ocean of life "rests" in its own surge, we will only embrace parts of it and resist the rest. Let's look at five simple examples of where—unknowingly—we are at war with the "waves of life."

We feel irritated each time:

1. The weather refuses to behave according to our wishes.
2. People around us fail to realize that our needs come first.
3. There is not supposed to be traffic at this hour!
4. People move like snails.
5. Someone tells us something about ourselves we don't want to hear.

Need life be this way? The answer is found in the following question: Can we ever hope to know the nature of real love, of its abiding peace, living from a false self that sees disturbances as its opportunity to get irritated? Is compassion or contentment possible for a nature that values being a victim? Clearly not; and yet, if we dare see it, we human beings are in a perpetual war with reality itself. We oppose any movement of life that seems to threaten our imagined sense of peace. Six and a half-billion people—all of us convinced that we know what should be happening in any given moment.

Yet, the evidence before us speaks louder than our protestations over it: we do not know what is "right." We only think we do because within us lives a nature that can, and always does, point to what is *wrong* with the moment before us. Such a mindset, supported by negative emotions that, in turn, nourish a victim mentality, can never know peace. To see the truth of this is the beginning of a new mind, one that is the same as the meditative life within which it finds the secret source of confidence, kindness, peace, and contentment.

Let Life Happen as It Must

At all times everything, everywhere, is unfolding as it must. *Getting stressed and struggling to change the outcome of any past event is like arguing with an echo to make it see your point of view.* In down-to-earth terms, to resent the person who cuts you off in traffic does nothing to change either that scary moment now passed or the sleeping nature of the one who endangered you. Yet, we believe that our negative reaction has something of a corrective nature to it. The truth is that negative reactions of any kind do not correct the condition seen as being at fault; they actually serve to continue that unwanted experience.

Let us ask ourselves: Have we ever made somebody like us by resisting his disapproving look? Wars don't end by fighting; fighting of any kind breeds the seeds of hatred and mistrust, whose harvest is always more conflict. Be assured: disapproving looks are always going to be on the faces of people for as long as they remain in the dark about the true purpose of life. But we can be different, providing we are willing to reconcile this extraordinary question:

What are we to do with what life brings to us—that we are sure just isn't "right"—especially when we can look out and see so many horrible things taking place on our planet? I am not saying we should disregard negative conditions, only that *things are the way they are* in the moment in which we see them unfold. And let there be no doubt about this: negative reactions make nothing better. In fact, we serve to accelerate the unwanted effect of any condition that we resist because—by our identification with it—we unknowingly become a part of what we don't want!

This much should be obvious: something that lives in the "dark" of us is hard at work, creating the illusion that the way to change or control what disturbs us is *to not want it.* But now we are shedding light on this negative nature (and its lies), which means our world can begin to grow brighter. So, let's summarize:

No moment can be different than it is; whether we like it or not means nothing, and our distaste for it changes nothing in what takes place before us. However, what does mean something is what we allow to happen within us in that moment, because as we are changed—by what we see about ourselves—*so changes the moment itself.*

When we speak of a "meditative life," we're saying not only that events are unfolding as they must, but that they also serve a higher purpose. Life itself, each of its "waves," is a kind of "window" through which we see what "is"—including the reality of how our awareness interacts and transforms all that is becoming moment to moment.

It's what we do inwardly—with what takes place outwardly—that alone has the power to transform both of these worlds in a way that's truly positive for all. And when we are aware of this truth, and its vital relationship with all that is taking place, we begin to see how our true human responsibility and the higher purpose of this life are really one movement. It's why our interior work to realize a fully meditative life is so important—crucial, really—to the enlightenment of human consciousness. Our world is transformed according to our ability to take part in it this way, just as we ourselves are transformed with the world as it reveals to us the truth of ourselves.

The universe is a work being continually perfected; though unseen, it is justice, compassion in action. Those who resist and resent what comes their way—who fight with its unending waves that rock their contrived sense of reality—are actually the ones who live without real choice. They must serve their struggle to resolve the sense of loss that comes each time the world changes without first having consulted them. So, instead of being what they could be—an intelligent instrument of a beautiful awareness that illuminates and transforms all it touches—these poor souls reflect ugliness in all its dark, malcontent forms. Such people have neither peace nor freedom. How can they? Any happiness built on a demand that life comply with its imagined pleasures is a disturbance waiting to happen. Yet, here's an astonishing truth: There is not one true reason to be unhappy, not one. How can this be? Let's review another important key lesson in life.

There is no moment in which everything around us isn't beginning. Can we look around us and see this truth? Can we see that the ocean of life—within whose endless waves we dwell—never stops beginning? Because, if we can see this fact, it means that whatever our mind tells us is the reason for our unhappiness is never the real reason for that pain. How can it be? The whole universe has changed since the passing of that moment our mind still holds responsible for its misery! What hasn't changed—and what resists change at the same time—is that lower level of our self that clings to negative images in order to hold onto its suffering! Which brings us to this grand question:

Will we choose to be a part of life's endless beginning? Shall we enter into the incorruptible present moment, or continue to live from a nature that clings to imagined endings so that it can complain about whatever disturbs that dream? Can we realize, as we have discovered, that everything that happens to us does so for the one purpose of revealing to us something of our present nature ... and, in so doing, invites us to transcend who we have been?

If we can answer these questions in the affirmative, then we stand at the threshold of a meditative life. We have entrance to the journey of all journeys because we can see the truth behind appearances: real life is self-renewing; and as we learn to align our will with this eternal principle, then a measure of its power—which is an aspect of God's life—becomes an active part of our own being. Let's look at one example of how this new and higher relationship with life might unfold in real time, under circumstances common to us all.

We are sitting someplace, or perhaps driving down the street, and something happens that creates a disturbance within us. Maybe it's something on the news, or someone touches an old nerve with a careless remark. It doesn't take much to stir up suffering, but now we know a better response than to wreck ourselves. In that same instant that we feel our world being "rocked"—instead of resisting that unwanted wave by setting out to "make things right"—we do nothing but let go, and watch the wave run through us. We don't fight life; we observe its movements. What does it mean to "watch" these waves, instead of letting them carry us away? Here's a crucial lesson in letting go:

Fighting with, resisting any wave creates more waves. Do something new: let that wave of worry or fear rise—and fall— back into the darkness from which it came; and be assured it will do just that, if we only agree to let it run its natural course.

Why should this non-action be our choice? Because if we dare to watch the wave go its own way, then soon we will observe a true miracle: all waves return—on their own—back into the uncharted depths of the ocean from which they came, but only when we watch and don't touch!

Our task is to no longer try to control or contain these waves, but to watch them come and go. We must learn how to use all of life's movements to free us from our false ideas that life can ever move against us. It cannot, any more than waves challenge the integrity of the ocean through which they move. In truth, the waves of the ocean—of life itself—refresh and renew the world of their origin. To know this is to cooperate with that greater consciousness that sits behind these changing forms.

See that everything in existence serves what is Good, and then choose to participate in life *as it is.*

The meditative life is an act of embracing the full moment through our awareness of it—whatever it brings. This level of watchfulness first sees what is real and then serves to "transform" it into the next and higher form of what is possible. This Divine process is perfect; it is eternal. Its promise is that we will know its being as our own if we will do the work of awakening to the truth of ourselves.

Adapted in part from the audio album
The Meditative Life

The First Step to Being Inwardly Still

KEY LESSON

Feeling sorry for yourself is like slipping off a boat at sea and, just as you're falling into the water, grabbing the anchor to take with you so you have something you can cling to in your time of trouble.

It was approaching the dead of winter when a spiritual teacher went walking through a deep mountain valley with three of his disciples. As it was very cold, the three students were worried about their teacher. They didn't want him to get sick, but none would speak up; all knew their teacher's insistence on privacy when it came to people sticking their nose into his personal affairs. But finally one of them could hold his peace no longer and spoke out:

"Teacher, it's not right that you don't have proper protection from this weather." And, gathering his courage, he went further.

"We all agree," he said as he looked over at his fellow students for a sense of support, "we want you to have a beautiful coat to help keep you warm."

The teacher understood the true nature of his students' protestations, but he also wanted them to learn the higher lesson of the moment: while it's good to have comforts, being without them is not important enough to despair over. Further, he wanted to show them the value of learning how to use whatever life supplies—or denies—them in the moment, but his brief words of instruction fell on deaf ears. Instead, his students insisted further:

"No, master, it's not right. We appreciate your modesty and your humility, but really, you need a nice warm coat. If you don't, you may catch your death of cold, and then what would become of us? Permit us to buy this for you, please?"

Continuing their conversation as they walked alongside a great river, all of a sudden they noticed a large fur coat floating downstream. One of the students exclaimed, "Look! It's a miracle! The Almighty has heard our prayers! How great is our fortune!"

The next moment—at their urging—the teacher dived into the cold waters to retrieve the fur coat as it floated along with the current. Another minute went by and the students were in shock: their teacher was being swept down the river along with the coat. But that wasn't all; it was obvious their teacher was in a great struggle of some kind. One by one they cried out, "Are you all right? What's wrong? Let go of the coat—you'll drown if you don't let it go!"

And from the distance they heard their teacher yell back to them, "I want to let go, *but it's not a coat!* It's a black bear ... and it won't let go of me!"

How many times a day do each of us "dive" headlong into that river of thoughts rushing through our own mind? Maybe it's to pull out of it some relief about a struggling relationship or some other personal concern, but the results seldom vary: we find ourselves in the same position as the teacher caught by the bear. In other words, we realize—too late—our true situation:

It isn't we who are holding onto what we thought would save us, but rather our own thoughts and feelings have a firm grip on us ... and they're dragging us under with them! Those who have ever struggled with any form of addiction have an intimate understanding of this reversal in roles: what was thought would save them—comfort or console them—is the very thing that betrays and then compromises them.

Our lives are filled with many such compromising moments, more than we're aware of. But generally speaking, only the most dramatic moments get our attention. It's then we realize, too late, we've become a captive of something that we thought would release us; "Out of the frying pan, into the fire," goes the old adage. We all know this familiar routine: the more we struggle to resolve our negative reaction, the more wrapped up in it we become. In other words, and returning to the wisdom story, the more we thrash about trying to escape the clutches of our personal "black bear"—that whirlpool of dark thoughts and feelings pulling us under—the deeper we sink into it.

The evidence is clear: struggling to save ourselves from a torrent of thoughts and feelings by adding more to them doesn't just diminish our chances to be free—it ensures we will only be swept further downstream by the very thing we reach for to save us. And we cannot stop thought any more than we can stop the fizz that shoots from a cola can when we accidentally drop it from our hand. Now, if we can see the truth of these things, the solution to our struggle—as surprising as it may seem at first glimpse—is right before our eyes. It's clear: *there's nothing left for us to do but to do nothing.* Please don't reject this discovery just because it doesn't make immediate sense to you. Let me explain the beautiful power and simplicity of what it means to "do nothing," and then you will see the power behind its truth.

All along, each and every life experience of ours has been trying to teach us—trying to reach us, right in the midst of our trials—this grand lesson: Liberation from our captive condition can't come by further deliberation of it any more than we can hope to repair a leaky faucet by buying a new plug for the sink. We see the wisdom in doing nothing toward our own troubled thoughts as we realize that *the only way not to be dragged under by our negative reactions to life is to stay out of their life.* This is a key idea: To mistake ourselves for any thought or feeling that moves through us is not unlike trying to measure the expanse of an open sky by using a breeze that's passing through it. Learning to "do nothing" means we don't jump into the river of thoughts as they rush by, even though it looks as though they carry with them what we need to be free. To "do nothing" means we meet any kind of conflicting movement within us with the one thing that can't be carried off by it: *stillness.*

Perhaps you've read the New Testament passage by Saint Paul, "In thy patience, possess ye your soul." Watchfulness is superior to willfulness because only by being still can we see—without a doubt—what is actually *our* will and what is not. Only by choosing to quietly stand on the bank of our own reactions as they rush by are we empowered to see that *who we really are* is not any one of our thoughts or feelings.

In many ways, this kind of watchfulness—our willingness to do nothing save be still in the face of our flooding reactions—is real meditation. Meditation isn't just sitting someplace with our eyes closed or quietly contemplating something of a spiritual nature. Meditation is a direct relationship with the sum of ourselves in the moment, where we stand as a witness to what moves through us instead of becoming its captive through our reaction to it.

If you say, "I don't know how to do that," consider this: How did you learn to eat? How did you learn to hold somebody's hand? How did you learn to appreciate a butterfly? How did you learn to love the wind? Your wish to know what you longed for created relationship with it. So, along with your awakening wish for greater interior freedom and peace, act out the truth you want to know.

When it's time to step back from some reaction that's tempting you to jump in—in order to get out of some jam—remember what you are learning here and have already seen as being true: "Been there, done that," the popular saying goes. Then take this completely new action: *do nothing but watch.* Be as still as you can be within yourself toward what you see there. This also means watching your own inability to be still. You need do nothing else for you to start seeing all that *isn't you*—meaning all that movement unfolding before your inner eyes: the fitfulness pulling you left and right, the sound and the fury of ten thousand thoughts and feelings coursing through you. Just watch it all. In no time you will understand the goodness of stillness; you'll know the magic that lends the true meditative life its mystery, its calm, and its unchallenged majesty.

Realize Your True Self in Stillness

KEY LESSON

Fearlessness comes with the birth of this new understanding: The only reason life changes as it does is to reveal the secret Goodness underlying those same changes.

To see a great mountain is to see the physical expression of a great principle. To see the expressed form of any such greatness is to stir in us the corresponding principle that already lives within us. This means that part of our pleasure as we gaze at a great mountain, or stand rapt watching an eagle in flight, is a momentary realization of our oneness with that great character we see before us. That power, that purity, such beauty had always been there, living within us, only we had been asleep to its indwelling presence. In this way, *nature reminds us that we have forgotten ourselves;* each time we see and are touched by the expression of some eternal principle, we catch a sweet glimpse of some aspect of our True Self. How nice.

Within each of us live nobility, kindness, gentleness, and the love that gives rise to all things timelessly good and true. The words used to describe these sentiments aren't important. They are meant only to help convey this special idea that the world we see with our eyes, the impressions we take from it, serve a greater purpose than is commonly known. The world exists as it does to help us realize that within us live the eternal principles that give rise to all the forms that we see; and, for our seeing this, to remind us—in turn—of this immeasurable truth: we are the Ground of all that we see. Your patient consideration of the following insights will help you see—for yourself—the facts behind this revelation.

The world we see with our eyes is secondary to the world within us that recognizes what it does, else we couldn't recognize it—we couldn't "know" it as we do when seeing it. The truth is, as modern physics now affirms, we never "see" anything—that is, we never have any feeling pass through our body, we never see a form of light, we never know a form of psychological darkness—whose existence isn't already a part of our consciousness, else we wouldn't be able to know it as we do in this moment.

This finding speaks of a world beyond anything we can imagine with thought, a higher realm within us that we're meant to be conscious of, but that we just don't know anything about. This amounts to a prince, a princess, living out their lives in the castle dungeon because they "forgot" they're entitled to live as royalty do.

This kind of forgetfulness is a timeless theme running through all classic spiritual literature. Whether it is the sleeping masses depicted in Eastern traditions, or the wakefulness or the watchfulness asked for by the Christ and Buddha, the case remains the same: perhaps we walk by a beautiful cherry blossom with its delicate fragrance budding on a tree, but we have no awareness of it. Its fleeting sweetness—meant to stir and awaken within us our interior counterpart of an everlasting sweetness—is lost to us. Why? We aren't there in the moment to receive the message.

We have lost the relationship between what we see with our eyes and the registration of it as an aspect of our own True Nature because we don't *see* what we see; instead *we think about what we see.* And when we think about what we see, what we receive is the content of thought that has stored that experience. We don't receive what is real, alive, changing, creative, and forceful. Instead, we dine upon ourselves, and it is a fool's feast.

There is one great principle that underpins a common thread found running through all world religions, because within it we find the secret foundation of all true religious experience. In Psalms 46:10 we are told, "Be still and know that I am God." Allow me to paraphrase this Divine invitation and ultimate spiritual instruction.

Be still: Cease from thinking about what you see, and *know*—
without thinking about it—that no real distance exists
between the seer and the seen. The beauty or ugliness
you see, near or far, is none other than Self.

and know: Realize that there is no real distinction between
what you perceive about something and what you receive
from it in the same moment. Life is a reflection of the
consciousness that reveals it. Nothing else exists outside
of this.

that I am God: I am not just the life source of all that has been
or ever will be seen, but I am the seer as well *that dwells
within you.* Your True Self is seer and seen at once.

What this teaches us is that a direct relationship exists between our potential to be still and what is possible for us to receive and realize about ourselves in that stillness. And there is no limit to these interior discoveries, because the depth and breadth of our True Self is without boundaries of any kind.

Ours is the gift to know that the universe we gaze at—the star-studded sky with its infinite galaxies—lives within us. Its ceaseless creation—*still* taking place in a continual genesis—is *ours* to midwife, nourish, and help see to its endless perfection. To be made "in the image of God" isn't just a sentimental idea; it is a Divine duty.

Whenever we quietly look up at a night sky and love the timeless feeling of it, what we really love is *being our timeless Self* for that moment. We couldn't love what was eternal unless something of that eternity was already living within us. We receive the love we give in that moment, and our world is made anew.

When we stand on the ocean shore, silently seeing the expansive waters spread out before us, we enter into their depths. Where is the true deep if not within the consciousness that reflects it? What is timeless, what is unfathomable does not reside outside of us. It dwells in the center of us; *it is our True Self.* We plumb the unknown worlds within ourselves, and the lands we explore are reclaimed by the Light that reveals them.

Stillness is the path of *revelation;* no other path to the truth of yourself exists, because the freedom you long to be is found only in one place: within your awareness of the evergreen flowering of God's life endlessly releasing itself through rebirth. True self-realization is the unending revelation of God's life as your own.

Be still and be free.

Adapted in part from the audio album
7 Steps to Oneness

SPECIAL KEY LESSONS IN REVIEW

1. It only seems as if there is something more important for you to do than to just quietly be yourself.

2. One way to avoid at least a few unpleasant conversations is to never again talk to yourself!

3. Silence is that silver cup that life fills over and over again without ever filling up.

4. Self-surrender is not the acceptance of our limitations, but the only true way to transcend them.

5. The only strength that never turns into its unhappy opposite is the higher self-understanding that you are not, and never have been, your weakness.

Chapter 7

BE ONE WITH THE LIGHT OF LIFE

Realize the Secret Treasure of
Your True Self

KEY LESSON

Every inspired thought—each new insight that points
to the heights of what we might yet become—serves to
enlarge the mind that conceives it. And the grand discovery
of that mind touched by any such truth is that within this
breaking light is found nothing less than the endlessness of
its own possibilities.

Each event and every moment of life brings with it a kind of
gift just for us, providing we will receive it. This priceless offer-
ing isn't about ways to empower ourselves through possessions
or greater position in life; it is presented to free us from the
stress and worry born of the false belief that such riches are the
road to realizing the value of our True Self.

What is this gift yet to be claimed? What power is there that
can make all of life's moments turn brightly golden? Please let
neither the simplicity nor the familiarity of the following answer
keep you from investigating the secret behind its unimaginable
promise: *Perfect love casts out fear.*

What is "perfect love"? To begin with, it is not an emotion
any more than a ray of light is the sun from which it emanates.
At present we know love—the highest order of ourselves—
through our experience of its various forms passing into and
through us; but much as a flute is not the notes that flow from
it, neither are any of the "sounds" of love that soothe the soul
the same as the perfect love for which it longs and seeks.

Think of a flower opening its soft petals to the welcoming
touch of the sun's morning light. Unfolding further, it collects

and passes this energy into the fruit growing there in its bud, giving it the food it needs to grow. Holding in mind this picture, see this fruit ripening and falling to the ground and how, in time, its seed becomes the stalk of another flower from which more fruit will be born. Now, as best you can, imagine all of these movements at once; realize that these seemingly individual expressions of life, death, and rebirth taking place in passing time are but one principle, eternally expressing itself, and you have some idea of what love is: nothing is made without its living Light, and all things are made new through its power.

Why does perfect love cast out fear, along with all of the ways that fear compromises us? Because much in the same way as it is impossible for a shadow to live in the light, perfect love ensures that dark divisive states such as fear, anxiety, and depression cannot dwell in the presence of its living Light. Our task, should we wish to walk through life with such a fierce advocate by our side, is to awaken ourselves to the fact of its presence as a power already within us. Where we can find this treasure of treasures—and how we can realize that our True Self is already one with it—*that's* the question! Let's find some real answers.

We can all see that life is a mystery. What remains unseen is how to solve it. But before we can ever hope to "solve" this enigmatic puzzle that we call our life, we must have all the pieces on the table; and there is one piece to this puzzle most people never find, because this missing piece is *our life* itself!

Life—this moment and every moment—is a school for the education of the soul. At its heart is an invisible core curriculum, a kind of celestial "program" with one great purpose: to help us realize that behind each of the life lessons that comes our way dwells a Divine, just, and loving Intelligence that wants us to be one with its life.

Imagine how different life would be if we understood that nothing happens to us that isn't sent our way to help us learn more about the eternal nature of love. With such a realization we would *know* that whatever takes place in our life has not come as something set against our best interests, but to help us realize them!

What prohibits us from awakening to this essential relationship and realizing its power as our own? In a word, resistance. We see life through the eyes of a part of us that instantly opposes whatever challenges its idea about the meaning of life and what's "best" for us in it. This false self refuses or denies anything that threatens the flattering image it has of itself. All in all, the negative effect of our unconscious condition can be stated like this: *We have become less intolerant.*

Something within us is creating a buffer of some kind—a barrier that stands between our need for liberation and the higher life lessons that help both catalyze and create this transformation of consciousness. Let's look at the two main reasons for this strange indwelling resistance that stands between us and the self-liberation for which we long, starting with the following short story. It's taken from a series of recorded talks entitled *Living Now.* Its lighthearted message points to a deep indwelling secret about our present level of Self, and its surprise ending gives us our first look at what stands between us and our right to be free.

Give Wings to Your Wish for Freedom

Once there was a little creature resting on the branch of a mighty Oak that was Father of the forest. The little creature was sitting there sighing, and from time to time crying a little bit—its tiny body almost buckling under some unseen weight. Finally the great old Oak could listen no longer. In a voice belonging to a giant, but that was also as gentle as a breeze, the mighty Oak spoke out:

"Little creature, what is wrong with you?"

The little creature was surprised to feel such concern coming from anyone, let alone the tree in which it was perched. But sensing the overwhelming kindness that came along with the question, it answered as best it knew to do. The words came fairly spilling out its mouth, as if a pent-up stream of water had been waiting to be released.

"Don't you see, that's just it ... I mean ... I'm not sure. Well, that's not entirely true."

"Whoa, slow down there little one," the Oak spoke in measured tones attempting to quiet the creature. "No need to be in a hurry telling me what you will. I've been standing here for centuries, so I'm not going anywhere. Can you be a little more specific about 'what' you're suffering over—and maybe then we can get to the 'why?' part of it?"

Somewhat becalmed by these words, the creature started over. "Well, no matter how I look at it, nothing makes sense. I mean ... I was sure it would be different than this."

The Oak considered this comment for a moment and asked the only question it could at that point: "What *exactly* was it that you thought would be so different?"

The little creature came out of its own thoughts for a moment as it realized the tree couldn't see what was so obvious to it.

"Why ... being a butterfly, of course. When I used to think about becoming a butterfly, I thought to myself my problems would be left behind me—beneath me, if you will ... but everything still irritates me. And," the little creature lowered its voice somewhat so as to be sure no one else would hear its next comment, "I'm afraid a lot of the time. I figured that after I had become a butterfly, I just wouldn't have the fears that I used to have, but I still do! And that's not all … the past—it bothers me! I was sure that as a butterfly my former life wouldn't be a problem for me anymore."

The tall Oak tree looked at the little creature and knew instantly what was wrong.

"Yes, I see; what you've said makes a lot of sense now. But, let me ask you a couple more questions. We both need to get to the bottom of this problem if we're going to solve this mystery for you." And the little creature said, "Oh, thanks so much!"

The Oak continued, "Do you find yourself getting tripped up quite often?"

The little creature thought for a minute and said, "You know what? I do get tripped up. Yes! I trip quite often as a matter of fact!"

"And how about this?" the tree followed up. "Do you spend a lot of time chewing over things?"

"Yes. I spend a lot of time chewing over things."

"And are there times when it takes you a long time to get out of your own way?"

The little creature was amazed at the accuracy of the tree's questions. "You've tagged it for me! All these things you said about me are true."

"Well," the great Oak spoke again. "I think I've figured out the mystery here. Are you sure you want to know the answer?"

"Of course I do," said the creature, somewhat surprised at the question. "Please go ahead."

"All right then," said the tree, carefully measuring out the medicine it knew would be bitter to the little creature clinging to its branch. "Here's the reason for your continuing confusion about why life isn't to your liking: you aren't a butterfly yet; you're *still a caterpillar.*"

If we hope to receive, realize, and be set free by the higher lessons that life prepares for us in all of our moments, we must bring ourselves into this story. It's worth noting here that wisdom tales, myths, and parables from every age share one thing in common: every character we meet in their stories lives within us; more accurately stated, we embody them, which is one of the reasons we find these truth tales so fascinating!

So, now we need to see what it is that we share in common with the little creature that can't understand its condition because it considers itself to be something it's not. By the way, within us also dwells the strength and wisdom of the great Oak, but we have yet to realize this as well!

The wise old tree knew—as we must come to see about ourselves if we would be free—that as long as the little caterpillar believed it was a butterfly, it would be bound to the Earth. Why is this true? Because in mistaking itself for what it *had yet to become*—a beautiful butterfly—it would refuse the life "lessons" required of it to complete its natural transformation. This reluctance to receive the shocks that we need is pretty much *our* condition as well. There are parts of our psychic system that reject the lessons needed for our evolution because they imagine they're already flying above the world of troubles. It is this mistaken sense of self that stands between us and true self-transformation. Which brings us to the second of the secret conditions that keeps us from realizing self-liberation.

Nothing that Resists Life Can Hope to Learn from It

Until we can embrace the lessons that ride into our lives on the back of events, we walk through an isolated world of our own making; confined and defined by the content of our own thoughts, we are cut off from reality. And, as long as we remain so, there is no hope of realizing our relationship with that limitless Light from out of whose life pours the lessons intended for our transformation.

So, this much is clear: something within us is acting against our best interests. But what would do this, and why? The following insight helps us to see why our "caterpillar consciousness"—our false self—resists the lessons we need in order to be born anew:

Real learning requires surrender.

Just as we saw how the caterpillar must let go of what it has been in order to realize the butterfly it's been created to become, so too we must yield to what is above us if our wish is to know its freedom as our own. This is the same higher lesson that Christ tried to teach his disciples when he washed their feet against their initial protests that he should not do so. His wish, which is the same as the wish of the Light he embodied, was to reveal the eternal relationship that exists between the greater and the lesser: the greater is continually pouring out its life, giving its light to the lesser. This means that *the lesser is made greater each time it surrenders to the greater,* because in that moment the lesser becomes the greater; then it understands that greater work of which it is now a part and to which it now wants to give itself again.

To give you a simple idea of this beautiful relationship, think of the way in which a barren winter grapevine yields itself to the first rays of a warm spring sun, drinking in the radiant energy that will—in a few months—be a part of the sweet fruit it grows. In nature we can see this order of relationship law: for one life to "increase," another must "decrease." The same holds true *within us.* We too must yield the still dark and undiscovered parts of ourselves to the light of awareness that transforms them, so that the soul can blossom and bear fruit. This eternal genesis is the secret nature of love, as is its living Light through which we perceive our relationship within it. Our gift in life, should we choose to receive it, is to witness and realize our oneness with this love that never betrays its lover.

As our inner eyes open, and we see that all things come to us for the sake of increasing our trust in this love, the flame of true faith ignites. By its light we see with ever-increasing clarity that nothing happens to us that isn't part of preparing us to transcend—to outgrow—who and what we have been. Our conviction in the goodness of Truth moves past all doubt, and our confidence grows that we've found what we've been looking for all our life. The Light for which we searched is real and now we know it. The first leg of the great Journey is made and now a new task is set before us: to *embody the Truth we have found,* to serve the celestial powers we once thought should be subjugated to serve us. Now our inner work is to *practice being one* with this Light whose love has made possible our awakening. The fruit of this union is freedom. Some call it enlightenment. By any other name it is joy. This Life is yours if you give it yours.

Solve the Mystery of Living in the Light

KEY LESSON

An artist's canvas is not the colors that have been played out across it, but rather it is their showplace. In much the same way our higher nature has nothing in common with the rainbow of thoughts and feelings always painting the sky of our present consciousness. True Self doesn't call itself bright or dull depending upon the dominant "shade" of the moment. It is always just Light.

We have all read books or seen animated movies in which, once the "humans" retire for the evening, everything in the kitchen or the child's playroom comes to life.

In Disney's *Beauty and the Beast,* the cups, dishes, and silverware are all special characters, each with a crucial role. Collectively they help to ensure that love blossoms between the two main characters whose transformation follows as wild flowers do the first spring rain.

In *Cinderella,* the mice, birds, and even a pumpkin act as a united force to thwart the selfish plans of a wicked stepmother and, in so doing, create the fairytale ending we all know and love. With these images in mind, the story you're about to read also has a very special ending designed to help you realize the secret treasure of your True Self. Let's set the scene:

It was time for bed on a cold New England night. The fire in the cooking stove had died out, and the coals in the hearth had cooled to embers. Everyone moved as quickly as they could to finish their evening chores; visions of snuggling beneath warm bedcovers hurried them along toward bed. And, as was the custom of this small New England family back in the late 1800s, the last one to retire—usually Dad—would snuff out all the candles except for the large one he carried with him on his appointed rounds. This biggest of all the candles would sit out the night—burning bright—in the middle of the kitchen for anyone who needed its light in the darkness of the wee hours. As was the custom back then, much as it remains today, the candle itself sat in a saucer-like holder with a handle for ease of carrying it around.

Now, for the story:

It was an unusually quiet night. Perhaps the new blanket of snow, the first of the season, had something to do with it ... but none of the usual conversation was going on in the kitchen. The tea cups that loved to gossip about the day's events were silent, and even the sink—whose habit it was to complain every night about the dishes left in it—had nothing to say. It was as though everyone was waiting for something to happen. Only what?

It was the candleholder that finally broke the silence. He was speaking to Ms. Wax—a part of the candle he was holding at the moment, and someone with whom he felt very close. He had always looked up to her as a consequence of their positions in life, but there was an edge to his voice that evening.

"Mind if I say something that's been on my mind?"

"That's never stopped you before!" said Ms. Wax, somewhat teasing him. Besides, she was grateful for the conversation. A moment or two went by without a further word from the candleholder. An unusual tension came over the room.

"I'm all ears," she said, thinking it would help break the ice. Besides, surely her quip would get a laugh. It had always been considered humorous among nonhuman beings to speak of themselves as having human features. Sure enough, a few chuckles came spilling out of the open cupboards above her; but the candleholder wasn't amused.

"I'm quite serious," he said a moment later. "There's something that's been bothering me ever since we were put together this way, and I have to get it off my chest." A few more laughs came from distant corners of the kitchen, but so intent on his conversation was he that the candleholder didn't even hear his own joke. And, for reasons unknown to himself, he fairly whispered what he had to say next.

"I'm jealous of the relationship you have with the flame, how you dance with it through the night so high above me. I have always wanted to know what it feels like to have it touch me the way it touches you." He paused there to consider his condition, so as to be clear. Then he went on:

"The only relationship I have with the warmth and light of the flame is the little bit of it that spills over the edge of your body to reach mine." He paused again—already uncertain whether he should have made this confession. So he waited for her to say something, but nothing came; the seconds that passed felt like an eternity. Surely, he thought to himself, I've made a fool of myself, but just as he was falling into a pool of dark thoughts her next words saved him.

"That's so strange," she said, "that you should tell me this now. You see I feel the same way that you do!"

"What on Earth are you talking about?" blurted out the candleholder, clearly irritated with her comment. "Every night you and Mr. Wick are joined together with the flame in a way I will never know. What can you possibly know of the isolation I endure down here below? I hold you both, and yet ... I have no direct relationship with the flame as you do."

"Oh," sighed Ms. Wax aloud, "if only you knew."

"Knew what?!" he retorted, growing even more impatient with her seeming insensitivity to his plight.

"What it's like to be me ...," she said in tones meant to melt his heart. "You wish you could be like me, but you don't know the half of it. Each night I pour myself into Mr. Wick so that the flame can burn true and bright, but it's not me who knows this light as you imagine I do. You see," she went on, measuring her words so that the candleholder might better understand her condition, "it's not me, but it's Mr. Wick that has it best of all. The flame may use me, but it takes him with it as it burns. His is the life; how I wish I was Mr. Wick!"

At that instant a third voice broke into their conversation, and it came from Mr. Wick himself. His words would have seemed rudely spoken under other circumstances, but his tone told them otherwise:

"Neither one of you understand what you're talking about." Their silence bid him to carry on.

"Yes, it's true: the flame dances all around me, consuming me as it does, but still I am not a part of it as you imagine. So you both have it all wrong: far from being at peace with my place in life, though I wouldn't change the way things are, the flame never really allows me to rest. And I think it's important for you to know that its beautiful light is more unknown to me than it is to you."

"What you say can't be true," said Ms. Wax.

"How is that possible?" said the candleholder almost at the same time.

"I doubt you will understand," said Mr. Wick, adding that he intended no insult. "But because of how close I am to it, *I am blinded by its light*. I can neither see it nor be with it as you imagine." And then, as if to finalize the conversation that, in truth, he felt was no one's business but his own, he said, "So, enough with what you wish you had and don't! I am no different from you. My longing to be one with the flame never stops burning."

Then something happened that had never happened before, at least as far as anyone knew. Such events had only been written about in stories. Yet ... there it was: *the flame itself began to speak*. As it did, a gentle light poured out from it, filling every corner of the kitchen; the whole room pulsated with the rhythm of its carefully chosen words.

"My friends ... Please listen to me. Stop your complaining. You know not what you say. *We all share the same wish*." The flame waited before it spoke further, taking the collective silence in the room as consent for it to continue on.

"Just as the three of you long to draw nearer to me, to this flaming body of mine that you can feel and see, so *I long to be one with the Light that grants me my life*." Again the flame paused. "Don't you see, my friends? What is true for you is true for me, which is why you are mistaken if you seek to draw nearer to me. *I am not the source of myself*—any more than a spring branch creates the fruit that grows on a tree. And there's something else you should know as well." The flame spoke in slow and carefully measured tones, indicating it was about to say something important:

"Without each of you—*as you are*—being and doing as only you can—we wouldn't even be having this conversation, would we? I know it's difficult to grasp, but we are all a part of the very thing we seek."

This story offers us a hint about what may be the greatest mystery of all. Christ spoke of it when he told his disciples, "For I tell you that many kings and prophets have desired to see those things which ye see, and have not seen them; and to hear those things which ye hear, and have not heard them" (Luke 10:24).

In the original Hebrew, the language spoken by Christ in his time, the meaning of these words—"to see those things which ye see"—is not what it seems at first glance. The first use of the word to *see* in this text doesn't mean to literally see something, as in an object perceived. In this instance the word indicates the idea that one receives direct knowledge—a personal understanding—of what is seen, as can only be granted by one's awareness of its invisible character.

In the second use of the word to *see* in this quotation, we find its common meaning: to look or gaze upon something, or someone (outside of yourself). So, the "hidden" story in this passage tells us two things: first, that Christ's disciples were awakening to a whole new kind of perception: they could "see" that in order to *know* real life—to take part in the perfection of the greater kingdom to which they were called—*they would have to be one with it.* They were coming to understand that this kind of higher seeing and true being were one and the same reality.

Within this same passage from Luke—"Many kings and prophets have desired to see those things which ye see, and have not seen them ...."—also shines the light of another great truth that is the secret message in the story about the candle and the flame: what we seek cannot be seen with our physical eyes nor dreamed of with thought. The only way to know the Light that never dies, that Love that is the unseen source of the flame we see and are drawn to, is *to become one with its Life.*

Now, as a necessary part of our work, let's examine how we can realize our inherent oneness with this indwelling Light— even as the flame in our story longed to know the Light of its source. To answer these questions concerning the achievement of an illumined life, we start with a strange discovery:

We read in the New Testament, and other timeless religious writings as well, that "taking thought" about tomorrow—searching for ways to enhance ourselves—can neither diminish our fears nor add anything of true value to our life; yet in these same teachings we find no real "how to" stop being identified with thoughts that trouble us about our future.

We also hear that one must have faith to move "mountains"—but again, no mention of "how to" call upon this power to clear the way before us. Now let's uncover why the enlightened ones never speak in terms of "how to" be free.

The word *mountain*—as used in this familiar passage of Christ's teaching—doesn't mean a physical barrier, as in something standing between us and a hoped-for position or possession we've imagined will bring us security and peace. The original Hebrew language implies that this "mountain"—that only faith can move out of our way—is not a physical barrier of any kind; it is more a psychological obstacle that "rises to meet (us)"—much as the way fear never enters into the picture of some new plan of ours *until* we imagine losing the reward that might come with it. Here we are taught that mountains are molehills of our own making that come into existence the moment we set out to increase ourselves in a time to come.

So faith is not a power meant to deliver us the worldly pleasures or treasures we imagine will set us free. Here we can see that real faith has nothing to do with wanting to possess or prevent anything. Its true nature is *a new order of freedom that comes with being able to see through the false idea* that who we really are *needs praise or possessions in order to be happy and whole.* In other words, as we realize that the contentment we long for already lives within us, we are empowered to tell that "mountain" of discontented thoughts and feelings to "move out of the way." It must obey our command. Let's examine this same important insight from a slightly different angle.

The real power behind faith is found *in the Light within us* that shows us what's true, and what's not, about who and what we are in reality. This insight helps explain the old adage that "the truth sets us free," because it means that in moments of trial our enlightened self-understanding actually "goes before us" to make the right choice for us! Rather than search outside ourselves for a solution to our suffering—as when we look for someone to tell our troubles to—or run after the promise of some new "power" to escape the shadow of a fear, we deliberately drop these old reactions in favor of quietly remembering what we know is true: there's nothing that we need to do to get past any dark shadow that shows up in our life except to *be the Light that already lives within us.* If we do our part, the rest is done for us.

Do try to see this oh-so-subtle truth that the flame in our story wanted to teach his friends. The candleholder, Ms. Wax, and Mr. Wick did not understand that they were already a part of the Light for which they longed; though the Light lived within them, they knew it not. The same holds true for us! *Nothing* is missing from our lives except for our not yet awakened ability to see this essential truth: just as fire needs wood to express its warmth and light, so too do we need the "darkness" of what we have yet to understand about ourselves. Let me explain this life-changing idea:

It rarely occurs to us, but *there is a greater potential in what we don't yet know about this life of ours than there is in what we've already seen about it.* So this great undiscovered territory—this "darkness" within us—is there for a distinctly Divine purpose: it exists as it does to serve the Light that reveals it; for in each such revelation there is a simultaneous realization and release of a new order of consciousness. There is such beauty in this idea, for it speaks to the possibility of a continual rebirth within us. What this means to us, and much to the heart of this book, is that we don't yet see "problems" for what they really are: *a part of the Light within us that we have yet to perceive!* Any thought or feeling that troubles us in mind or heart, any fear or worry, is like *a candle not yet lit.* What purpose has any flame or light—in any form we may find it—other than to enter into and transform what is dark into more of itself?

For instance, maybe we turn around one day and find ourselves caught in the dark grip of some kind of fear. Perhaps we see the one we love "looking the other way"; maybe a phone call delivers uncertain news about our deteriorating health; or someone tells us about a forthcoming change at work that threatens our sense of security.

In moments such as these, our future grows dark as it seems full of the loneliness, worry, and loss we see coming our way.

But our lives need not be swallowed up in unconscious servitude to this kind of suffering. We have another choice *if* we will only dare be still and be the Light. Here now are some ways to practice realizing the truth of your Self. Each case begins with remembering to make the new choice that follows:

- Instead of surrendering yourself to its punishing presence, bring your loneliness into the Light of your Self. If you will remain there within your awareness of this "darkness," here's what you'll see take place before your inner eyes: the fear of being alone will be transformed into the contentment of *knowing* that you have never been without the love that you long for. You will see that a tenderness beyond words lives within the Light you have embraced.
- Bring your fear and worry about "tomorrow" into the Light of your Self. Remain there in your awareness of these frightening shadows, and here's what you'll see unfold before your inner eyes: you'll watch these dark doubts dissolve into an unquestioned *knowing* that no time to come has power over the peace of being in the present moment. You will see that serenity is one with the life of the Light you have chosen to be.
- When visited by some sense of loss or emptiness, bring it into the Light of your Self. Remain quietly attentive to how that dark state wants to drag you into its world, even as you hold it in your awareness, and you'll see a miracle take place before your inner eyes: that feeling of being forsaken will be transformed into the fullness of *knowing* that who you really are is wholeness itself.

For your willingness to be inwardly watchful, you will see that the Light of your Self reaches everywhere in the universe ... so how could you ever be alone? All that lives ... lives within the Light of your Self.

After many years of talking to aspirants about *being the Light* instead of searching for what they think they need to deal with their dark states, I have found there is one main reason most people won't take the leap of releasing their fears into the Light that lives within them. They profess a love of the Light, but whenever an unwanted moment appears, and they look into its unknown abyss ... they see no Light there, only darkness. Then comes an immediate resistance, and darkness rules the day. Let me shed some light on this problem. Things are not always as they are seen.

Do you recall the wonderful characters in *The Wizard of Oz*? Along with Dorothy—who was trying to find her way back home—there were the Scarecrow, the Tin Man, and the Cowardly Lion: her compatriots on the journey to see the great wizard who would grant each of them their most fervent wish.

The scarecrow wanted a brain, a mind with which to reason and know the truth of things. The tin man hoped for a heart to beat in his hollow tin chest, so that by its warmth and rhythmic beating he would know the presence of the love for which he longed; and the cowardly lion wanted courage to face his fears, to meet any form of darkness with what it takes to defeat it. By the end of the story—largely as a result of what they go through because of their love for Dorothy—each makes this glad discovery: the very quality of character for which they had gone out searching was already living within them!

So it is with us: *we have forgotten that who we really are cannot be made a captive of any dark condition any more than a sunbeam can be caught and held in a bottle.* Our True Self is success itself, in every meaning of the word, because by its Light it fulfills and liberates all that it touches.

Never mind all the voices you'll no doubt hear shouting at you the first time you decide to be the Light of your Self. That which is dark does not go gently through being made new and bright. So there is work involved. But unlike all our former achievements that we see crumble beneath us even as we mount them for a temporary high, the Light we realize within us never fails; it literally carries us above whatever mountain is before us by revealing it to be nothing other than what we had yet to see about ourselves.

We cannot control the way the world turns, we cannot change day into night, we cannot keep what is not ours; and we cannot hide these facts from ourselves, no matter how hard we try. But what we are given to do, and that turns out to be the one power of ours truly capable of transforming the whole of life, is that we can choose—moment to moment—to be the Light of our Self. We are created as co-creators of all that we can be conscious of within ourselves. It is our right to be in relationship with only those powers whose presence serves our chosen purpose in life ... which is to be one with the Light.

SPECIAL KEY LESSONS IN REVIEW

1. Yes, "all good things must come to an end," but this is only half the story. It's equally true that what is Good in life is always just beginning.

2. Real fearlessness comes with knowing that you have everything you need to succeed in the same moment that it's needed.

3. When it comes to "What should I do?" about the painful negative states we see in ourselves, here is all we need to know: what is condemned remains concealed; what is concealed never heals.

4. Real love cannot be deceived because it wants nothing outside of itself.

5. Into each of our lives comes some fight that must be made; however, the key to true self-victory is not that we "win" at all costs, but rather that we always choose in favor of the Light that ensures we remain true, kind, and innocent in spite of the cost.

SUMMARY OF A STORY
WITHOUT END

What is Truth?
> *But the moment revealed.*

What is Light?
> *But God concealed.*

Sources

Beyond Dependency, 2001: published by Life of Learning Foundation.

Design Your Destiny, 1999: original publisher, Llewellyn Publications. Now published by Life of Learning Foundation.

The Illusion of Limitation, 2005: audio album, published by Life of Learning Foundation.

The Intimate Enemy, 1997: original publisher, Llewellyn Publications. Now available in revised version, *Who Put That Stone in My Shoe?* 2004, published by Life of Learning Foundation.

Let Go and Live in the Now, 2004: published by Red Wheel/Weiser.

Living Now, 2005: audio album, published by Life of Learning Foundation.

The Lost Secrets of Prayer, 1998: original publisher, Llewellyn Publications. Now published by Life of Learning Foundation.

The Meditative Life, 2005: audio album, published by Life of Learning Foundation.

The Secret of Letting Go, 1990: published by Llewellyn Publications. New revised and expanded edition, 2007: Llewellyn Publications.

7 Steps to Oneness, 2006: audio album, published by Life of Learning Foundation.

About Life of Learning Foundation

Life of Learning is a nonprofit organization founded by author Guy Finley in 1992. Its foremost purpose is to help individuals realize their true relationship with life through higher self-studies. The foundation is operated and run solely by volunteers. Everyone is welcome.

Guy Finley speaks three to four times each week at the foundation to the men and women who gather there to learn more about self-realization. Everyone is invited to share in the powerful transformational atmosphere that permeates each insight-filled talk. Each meeting awakens new energies, deepens intuitive powers, heals past hurts, and delivers welcome relief.

Life of Learning Foundation, located in the community of Merlin, Oregon, near the city of Grants Pass, rests in the heart of southern Oregon's most beautiful country. Visitors enjoy fourteen acres of old-growth sugar pine, beautiful flower gardens, organic foods, and walking trails with special places for meditation along the way. Whether you enjoy wild rivers, scenic lakes, or mountain hiking, you're only minutes away from nature at its best. Twice a year, the foundation hosts special retreats for visitors during the third weeks of December and June. The June "Talks in the Pines" event is an annual favorite.

Visit *www.guyfinley.org* to learn more about Guy's work, the Life of Learning Foundation, and for a wealth of helpful information, free audio and video downloads, and to request your free starter kit.

A Special Gift for You
Free DVD

The Power to Never Again Feel Powerless from best-selling author Guy Finley. A special gift for buyers of *The Essential Laws of Fearless Living*. Includes FREE shipping.*

Discover the natural authority that lies deep within you—a living presence that knows exactly how to handle any difficult moment and use every experience to reach increasing degrees of effortless self-command.

Learn the secrets of living a higher, happier, more meaningful life in the special 60-minute DVD *The Power to Never Again Feel Powerless*. In it, you will discover the amazing possibilities of a life without limits:

- Happiness with no strings attached
- Peace of mind that can't be compromised
- Relationships without fear or compromise
- An unbreakable sense of safety and security
- Confidence to accept any challenge life brings
- A Love that leaves no one out of its embrace

Everything you need to know about the Source of true self-liberation is available now. Don't miss out! Get your FREE copy of *The Power to Never Again Feel Powerless* by author Guy Finley today.

Visit *www.guyfinley.org/LawsDVD* or call (541) 476-1200 to request your FREE DVD today!

* Free shipping offer valid for addresses in the U.S. only. Limited time offer. Subject to change. Please visit the Web site above for further information and restrictions.

About the Author

Guy Finley, founder and director of Life of Learning Foundation, has been showing people how to find a life of uncompromised freedom and enduring fulfillment for 30 years. He is the best-selling author of more than 35 books and audio programs, including *The Secret of Letting Go* and *Let Go and Live in the Now*. Guy Finley is a modern-day master, who teaches us to live in the light of our own True Selves, to let go of fear, and to know the true power that comes with realizing the higher purpose of life. He lives in Oregon. Visit him online at *www.guyfinley.org* and subscribe to his free weekly e-newsletter.

To Our Readers

Weiser Books, an imprint of Red Wheel/Weiser, publishes books across the entire spectrum of occult and esoteric subjects. Our mission is to publish quality books that will make a difference in people's lives without advocating any one particular path or field of study. We value the integrity, originality, and depth of knowledge of our authors.

Our readers are our most important resource, and we appreciate your input, suggestions, and ideas about what you would like to see published. Please feel free to contact us, to request our latest book catalog, or to be added to our mailing list.

Red Wheel/Weiser, LLC
500 Third Street, Suite 230
San Francisco, CA 94107
www.redwheelweiser.com